First World War
and Army of Occupation
War Diary
France, Belgium and Germany

18 DIVISION
53 Infantry Brigade
Queen's Own (Royal West Kent Regiment)
7th Battalion
1 February 1918 - 30 April 1919

WO95/2040/2

The Naval & Military Press Ltd
www.nmarchive.com
Published in association with The National Archives

Published by

The Naval & Military Press Ltd

Unit 10 Ridgewood Industrial Park,

Uckfield, East Sussex,

TN22 5QE England

Tel: +44 (0) 1825 749494

www.naval-military-press.com

www.nmarchive.com

This diary has been reprinted in facsimile from the original. Any imperfections are inevitably reproduced and the quality may fall short of modern type and cartographic standards.

© **Crown Copyright**
Images reproduced by permission of The National Archives, London, England, 2015.

Contents

Document type	Place/Title	Date From	Date To
Heading	WO 2040/2		
Heading	18th Division 7th Bn Q.O. Roy. West Kents Jan 1918 Apl 1919 From 55 Bde 18 Div		
War Diary	Houthulst		
War Diary	Herzeele	01/02/1918	09/02/1918
War Diary	Mondescourt	10/02/1918	16/02/1918
War Diary	Caillouel	17/02/1918	25/02/1918
War Diary	Frieres 2 Camp.	26/02/1918	26/02/1918
War Diary	In The Line	27/02/1918	12/03/1918
War Diary	Ly Fontaine	13/03/1918	19/03/1918
War Diary	In The Line	20/03/1918	22/03/1918
War Diary	Rouez	23/03/1918	23/03/1918
War Diary	In The Line	23/03/1918	27/03/1918
War Diary	Mantebray	28/03/1918	31/03/1918
Miscellaneous	Officers Issued During Month.	10/03/1918	10/03/1918
Miscellaneous	Appendices 79, 80, 81 and 82.		
Operation(al) Order(s)	Cider. Order No. 88 App 79	06/03/1918	06/03/1918
Miscellaneous	Battalion Provisional Defence Scheme. Battalion In Brigade Reserve. App 80	10/03/1918	10/03/1918
Operation(al) Order(s)	7th Battalion Royal West Kent Regiment. Order No. 89 App 81	11/03/1918	11/03/1918
Operation(al) Order(s)	7th Battalion Royal West Kent Regiment. Order No. 90 App 82	18/03/1918	18/03/1918
Heading	53rd Inf. Bde. 18th Div. War Diary 7th Battn. The Royal West Kent Regiment. April 1918 Attached : Appendices 83, 84 & 85		
War Diary	Gentelles	01/04/1918	01/04/1918
War Diary	Line	01/04/1918	05/04/1918
War Diary	Gentelles	06/04/1918	06/04/1918
War Diary	Line	07/04/1918	08/04/1918
War Diary	Gentelles	09/04/1918	09/04/1918
War Diary	Line	10/04/1918	10/04/1918
War Diary	Gentelles	11/04/1918	11/04/1918
War Diary	Line	12/04/1918	13/04/1918
War Diary	St. Fuscien	14/04/1918	25/04/1918
War Diary	Boyes	26/04/1918	26/04/1918
War Diary	Saleux	27/04/1918	27/04/1918
War Diary	Cavillon	28/04/1918	28/04/1918
War Diary	Metigny	29/04/1918	30/04/1918
Miscellaneous	Officers Reinforcement During Month	01/04/1918	01/04/1918
Miscellaneous	Appendices 83, 84 and 85.		
Miscellaneous	7th Battn. Royal West Kent Regiment. Narrative of Operations. 1/22 April 1918 App 83	16/04/1918	16/04/1918
Operation(al) Order(s)	7th Batt Ryl West Kent Regt. Operation Order No. 2 Appendix 84	23/04/1918	23/04/1918
War Diary	7th Battalion Royal West Kent Regiment 53rd Infantry Brigade	24/04/1918	24/04/1918
War Diary	Metigny	01/05/1918	05/05/1918
War Diary	Montigny	06/05/1918	07/05/1918
War Diary	Behencourt.	08/05/1918	08/05/1918

Type	Description	Start	End
War Diary	Line	09/05/1918	23/05/1918
War Diary	Warloy	24/05/1918	25/05/1918
War Diary	Near Contay	26/05/1918	31/05/1918
War Diary			
Operation(al) Order(s)	7th Battn Royal West Kent Regt. Order No. 4 App 86	04/05/1918	04/05/1918
Operation(al) Order(s)	7th Battn Royal West Kent Regt. Order No. 5 App 87	06/05/1918	06/05/1918
Miscellaneous	7th Battn R W Kents Defence Scheme App 91		
Operation(al) Order(s)	7th Battalion R W Kent Regt Operation Order No 9 App 92	14/05/1918	14/05/1918
Operation(al) Order(s)	7th Battn. R.W. Kent Regt. Operation Order No 11 App 93	15/05/1918	15/05/1918
War Diary	Nr. Contay	01/06/1918	01/06/1918
War Diary	In The Line	02/06/1918	04/06/1918
War Diary	Near Warloy	05/06/1918	08/06/1918
War Diary	In The Line	09/06/1918	30/06/1918
War Diary	Honours And Awards.	12/04/1918	12/04/1918
War Diary	In the Line	01/07/1918	12/07/1918
War Diary	Warloy	12/07/1918	12/07/1918
War Diary	St. Pierre-A-Gouy	13/07/1918	31/07/1918
War Diary	Officers Joined During The Month.	00/07/1918	00/07/1918
War Diary	Near La Houssoye	01/08/1918	13/08/1918
War Diary	Nr. Henencourt	14/08/1918	18/08/1918
War Diary	Nr. Warloy	19/08/1918	31/08/1918
Miscellaneous	Officers' Joined During The Month	00/08/1918	00/08/1918
Operation(al) Order(s)	7th. Battalion Royal West Kent Regiment. Operation Order No. 23 App 123	06/08/1918	06/08/1918
Operation(al) Order(s)	7th. Battalion Royal West Kent Regiment. Operation Order No. 21 App 124	05/08/1918	05/08/1918
Map	Map C		
Miscellaneous	Attack With Artillery Barrage And Tanks.		
Miscellaneous	Narrative Of Attack On 8/8/18 App 125	08/08/1918	08/08/1918
Operation(al) Order(s)	Operation Order No. 30 App 125A	10/08/1918	10/08/1918
Operation(al) Order(s)	7th Battn Royal West Kent Regt Operation Order No 31 App 126	11/08/1918	11/08/1918
Operation(al) Order(s)	7th Battn Royal West Kent Regt. Operation Order No. 32 App 127	14/08/1918	14/08/1918
Operation(al) Order(s)	Operation Order No 33 7th Battn Royal West Regt App 127A	16/08/1918	16/08/1918
Operation(al) Order(s)	7th Battn Royal West Kent Regt Operation Order No. 34	17/08/1918	17/08/1918
Miscellaneous	7th Battalion Royal West Kent Regiment. Warning Order. App 129	21/08/1918	21/08/1918
Operation(al) Order(s)	7th Battalion Royal West Kent Regiment. Operation Order No 36 App. 129A	22/08/1918	22/08/1918
Miscellaneous	7th Battalion Royal West Kent Regiment. App 130	23/08/1918	23/08/1918
Miscellaneous	7th Battalion Royal West Kent Regiment. App 131	24/08/1918	24/08/1918
Miscellaneous	7th Battalion Royal West Kent Regiment. App 132	26/08/1918	26/08/1918
Miscellaneous	7th Battalion Royal West Kent Regiment. App 132A	27/08/1918	27/08/1918
Operation(al) Order(s)	Operation Order No 42 App 133	28/08/1918	28/08/1918
Operation(al) Order(s)	Operation Order No 44 App 134	29/08/1918	29/08/1918
War Diary	Operation Order No 50 App 135	30/08/1918	30/08/1918
War Diary	In The Line	01/09/1918	04/09/1918
War Diary	Nr. Montauban	05/09/1918	16/09/1918
War Diary	Aizecourt Le-Bas	17/09/1918	17/09/1918
War Diary	St. Emilie Line.	18/09/1918	24/09/1918
War Diary	Line.	24/09/1918	25/09/1918

War Diary	Gurlu Wood	26/09/1918	26/09/1918
War Diary	Maurepas	27/09/1918	28/09/1918
War Diary	Nurlu	29/09/1918	30/09/1918
Miscellaneous	Officer Casualties During Month	04/10/1918	04/10/1918
Miscellaneous	Narrative of Attack on 1st. September, 1918		
Miscellaneous	Narrative of Attack on 1st. September. 1918 App 136	01/09/1918	01/09/1918
Operation(al) Order(s)	7th. Battalion Royal West Kent Regiment. Operation Order No. 54 App 138	15/09/1918	15/09/1918
Miscellaneous	7th Battalion Royal West Kent Regiment. App 139	17/09/1918	17/09/1918
Miscellaneous	Movement. Order. 7th Battalion Royal West Kent Regiment. App 146	28/09/1918	28/09/1918
War Diary	Line.	01/10/1918	02/10/1918
War Diary	Cardonnette	03/10/1918	13/10/1918
War Diary	Cardonnette	14/10/1918	20/10/1918
War Diary	Line	21/10/1918	29/10/1918
War Diary	Bousies	30/10/1918	31/10/1918
War Diary	Officers' Joined During The Month.	00/10/1918	00/10/1918
Miscellaneous	7th. Battalion Royal West Kent Regiment. Battle Narrative. App 154		
Miscellaneous	7th Battalion Royal West Kent Regiment. Battle Narrative App 158		
War Diary	Line	01/11/1918	06/11/1918
War Diary	Le Cateau	07/11/1918	13/11/1918
War Diary	Premont	14/11/1918	30/11/1918
War Diary	Officers Casualties During The Month	04/11/1918	04/11/1918
Miscellaneous	2nd Bar To The Military Cross	07/11/1918	07/11/1918
War Diary	Premont	01/12/1918	31/12/1918
War Diary	Honours And Reward During The Month.		
War Diary	Premont.	01/01/1919	20/01/1919
War Diary	Bertry	21/01/1919	31/01/1919
Operation(al) Order(s)	7th. Battalion Royal West Kent Regiment. Operation Order No. 90 App 162	19/01/1919	19/01/1919
War Diary	Bertry.	01/02/1919	01/03/1919
War Diary	Clary	02/03/1919	31/03/1919
Operation(al) Order(s)	7th. Battalion Royal West Kent Regiment. Operation Orders No. 91 App 163	28/02/1919	28/02/1919
War Diary	Clary.	01/04/1919	30/04/1919

18TH DIVISION

7TH BN Q.O.ROY.WEST KENTS

JAN 1916 - APL 1919

From 55 Bde 18 Div

Army Form C. 2118.

Vol 23

WAR DIARY
or
INTELLIGENCE SUMMARY.
(Erase heading not required.)

Instructions regarding War Diaries and Intelligence Summaries are contained in F. S. Regs., Part II. and the Staff Manual respectively. Title pages will be prepared in manuscript.

Place	Date	Hour	Summary of Events and Information	Remarks and references to Appendices

Army Form C. 2118.

WAR DIARY
or
INTELLIGENCE SUMMARY.
(Erase heading not required.)

Instructions regarding War Diaries and Intelligence Summaries are contained in F. S. Regs., Part II. and the Staff Manual respectively. Title pages will be prepared in manuscript.

Place	Date	Hour	Summary of Events and Information	Remarks and references to Appendices

WAR DIARY
or
INTELLIGENCE SUMMARY.
(Erase heading not required.)

Army Form C. 2118.

4 Queens Kents

Place	Date	Hour	Summary of Events and Information	Remarks and references to Appendices
HERZEELE.	1-2-18.		Training under Company arrangements.	
	2-2-18.		Training as per Programme.	
	3-2-18.		Divine Services. 89. O.R. Reinforcements arrived.	
	4-2-18.		Training. Presentation of Decorations, including "1914 Star", by Brigade Commander. DIVISIONAL	App. 72.
	5-2-18.		Training during morning. Divisional "Fair" and Sports, near HERZEELE.	
	6-2-18.		Training as per Programme. Range Practices.	
	7-2-18.		Training as per Programme.	
	8-2-18.		Battalion moved from HERZEELE Area to NOYON, by train, marching thence to MONDESCOURT.	App. 73.
	9-2-18.		Hour of Start :- 4.0 p.m. 8th Feb. Arrived in Billets 3.0 p.m. 9th Feb. Transferred to 53rd.I.Bde.	
MONDESCOURT.	10-2-18		Cleaning-up Parades. 190.O.R. Reinforcements arrived (posted from 3/4 R.W.Kent Regt)	
	11-2-18.		Parades under Company arrangements. Training of Specialists. Inspection of Draft by C.O.	
	12-2-18.		Parades under Company arrangements. Training of Specialists.	
	13-2-18.		Parades under Company arrangements. Training of Specialists.	
	14-2-18.		Parades as per Programme. Baths.	
	15-2-18.		Parades as per Programme. Training of Specialists.	
	16-2-18.		Battalion moved by road to CAILLOUEL. Hour of start :- 11.15 a.m. Arrived in billets 1.30 p.m.	App. 74.
CAILLOUEL.	17-2-18.		Divine Services.	
	18-2-18.		Parades as per Programme. Range Practices.	App. 75.
	19-2-18.		Parades as per Programme. Range Practices.	
	20-2-18.		Parades as per Programme. Range Practices.	
	21-2-18.		Parades as per Programme. Range Practices.	
	22-2-18.		Parades as per Programme. Range Practices. Special attention to Anti-gas drill.	
	23-2-18.		Parades as per Programme. Range Practices. Inspection of 2- Coys., by 2nd in Commd.	
	24-2-18.		Divine Services.	
	25-2-18.		Battalion moved to HAUTE TOMEELE AREA (FRIERES CAMP) by road. Hour of start 10.30 a.m. Arrived 1.30 p.m.	App. 76. 77
FRIERES) CAMP.)	26-2-18.		Battalion relieved 7th Battn.K.R.R.C., in Southern Sub-sector of Northern sector, 18 Div. front.	
			Hour of Start :- 3.0 p.m. Relief complete 12.0 midnight.	
IN THE LINE.	27-2-18.		Battalion holding Line. Liaison patrols.	App. 78.
	28-2-18.		Battalion holding Line. Enemy Artillery above normal. Support trench at I.26.d.25.09 shelled heavily. Night patrols. Continuous work on trenches, dug-outs, wire etc.	

Army Form C. 2118.

WAR DIARY
or
INTELLIGENCE SUMMARY.
(Erase heading not required.)

Instructions regarding War Diaries and Intelligence Summaries are contained in F.S. Regs., Part II. and the Staff Manual respectively. Title pages will be prepared in manuscript.

Place	Date	Hour	Summary of Events and Information	Remarks and references to Appendices
			OFFICERS JOINED DURING THE MONTH.	
			(Lieut.) A/Capt. E.WATTS)	
			(Lieut.) A/Capt. F.C.LOVETT.) Posted from 3/4	
			2nd.Lieut. H.P.RIMINGTON.) Battn.R.W.Kent (Joined 10-2-18.	
			2nd.Lieut. G.M.HEAPHY.) Regt. (	
			2nd.Lieut. C.M.HOLMES.) (	
			2nd.Lieut. K. BLEW. -do- Joined 16-2-18.	
			2nd.Lieut. J.F.HEATLY. -do- Joined 20-2-18.	
			2nd.Lieut. S.H.WEBB. -do- (Not yet joined.)	
			OFFICERS' CASUALTIES DURING THE MONTH.	
			2/Lieut. P.D.GAUSDEN. Proceeded on 6-months Tour of Duty in England 9-2-18.	
			Lieut. G.L.MISKIN. Transferred to England, Sick, 14-2-18.	
			HONOURS & AWARDS.	
			Belgian "Croix-de-Guerre" :- 24796. C.S.M. Naylor.I.	
			24770. Pte. Tucker.J.	
			18382. Cpl. Patchin.R.C.	
			-----------------000-----------------	
Field.	6-3-18.			

CR Crummond Lieut.Col.
Commanding 7th Battalion Royal West Kent Regiment.

WAR DIARY
INTELLIGENCE SUMMARY

Army Form C. 2118.

7th R. West Kents
March 1916

Place	Date	Hour	Summary of Events and Information	Remarks and references to Appendices
IN THE LINE	1-3-16		Battalion holding line - Southern sub sector of Northumberland. 18th Divisional front. "A" Coy front line left; "C" Coy front line right.	
"	2.3.16 / 3.3.16		Battalion holding line. Reorganisation of positions; building & improvement of Strong Points. M.G. Emplacements &c.	
"	6.3.16		Battalion holding line. Inter Company relief. "B" in left front; "D" in right front; "A" Coy in support; "C" Coy in reserve.	App 79
"	8.3.16 / 10.3.16		Battalion holding Line. Improvement, strengthening & putting of posts. Battalion personnel supplied with for work outside in Brigade Reserve vivid.	App. 20
"	11.3.16		Battalion holding Line. Inter coy relief & rebuilding of Strong Points.	
"	12.3.16		Battalion relieved by 10th Battn Essex Regt, right of 13/3 March, incomplete night patrolling before relief.	App 81
LY FONTAINE	13.3.16		Battalion in Brigade Reserve at LY FONTAINE (D'Coy at REMIGNY). Daily work on strengthening & improving MG emplacements; furnishing Stony Point with 3 days supply of water & rations.	
	6		Daily working parties under direction of 79th Field RE.	
	18.3.16		Battn at REMIGNY. 14th and 16th	
	19.3.16		Enemy aeroplane forced down in our lines at about 6.05 am. Pilot was taken prisoner.	

Army Form C. 2118.

WAR DIARY
or
INTELLIGENCE SUMMARY.
(Erase heading not required.)

Instructions regarding War Diaries and Intelligence Summaries are contained in F.S. Regs., Part II. and the Staff Manual respectively. Title pages will be prepared in manuscript.

Place	Date	Hour	Summary of Events and Information	Remarks and references to Appendices
LY FONTAINE	19.3.18		and sent to Battalion under escort. Battalion relieved 13th Battn Essex Regt. in Southern Subsector of Northern Sector of 18th Divisional Front, night of 19th/20th. Lieut Col J.D. CROUTHWAITE M.C. resumed Command of Battalion, vice Lt Col G.H. CINNAMOND	
IN THE LINE	20.3.18		Battalion Lewisenberg in near MOY. "Standing to". Information received that enemy was massing in large numbers	
	21.3.18		Under cover of dense mist enemy advanced & surrounded Battn HQ at about 11.0 am. 'A' 'B' and 'C' Coys were also surrounded at about 10.30 am. Capt A.V. McDONALD M.C. 2nd in command was sent to Brigade HQ at about 9.0 am. From there he gathered remnants of Battalion, and all available reinforcements (which had been sent from "Details" at FRIERES CAMP), and took over command. Battn gradually withdrew to FAILLOUEL and held BLUE LINE just West of Canal. Approximate casualties – 20 officers & 577 OR. In addition, personnel from 18th Div Wing III Corps RTC had been sent to various parts of the front, together with personnel from Corners to Bridgeheads position of front also become casualties.	
	22.3.18		Battn withdrew to former Divnl HQ at ROUEZ during night 22/23	
ROUEZ	23.3.18		In Divisional Reserve. Fell back on evening on VILLEQUIER AUMONT taking up line running	

T2134. Wt. W708—776. 500000. 4/16. Sir J.C. & S.

Army Form C. 2118.

WAR DIARY
or
INTELLIGENCE SUMMARY.
(Erase heading not required.)

Instructions regarding War Diaries and Intelligence Summaries are contained in F.S. Regs., Part II. and the Staff Manual respectively. Title pages will be prepared in manuscript.

Place	Date	Hour	Summary of Events and Information	Remarks and references to Appendices
IN THE LINE.	23.3.18		Quiet WEST of CHAUNY, joining up with 9th Leicesters & 3rd in the Village (2 casualties)	
	23/24.3.18		Withdrew to COMMENCHON	
	24/25.3.18		Held CREPIGNY Line, took fell back & retiring on MONDESCOURT, holding hill West of Village. Then fell back behind BAOEUF (8 casualties on 24th) (37 Casualties on 25th)	
	25/26.3.18		During night fell back on POINT OISE & billeted for night	
	26.3.18		At 10.0 am marched to CAISNES. Rested. Started 5.0 pm; then moved to NAMPCEL where night was spent	
	27.3.18		At 2.0 pm moved from NAMPCEL via AUTRECHES to MANTEGRAY where Details & Transport joined at 7.30 pm	
MANTEGRAY.	28.3.18		Resting & cleaning up	
	29.3.18		At 4.0 am Battn. marched off & bussed lorries at 6.30 am. Proceeded to BOVES, arriving at 6.30 am, 30th. Bivouaced and moved to SENTELLES immediately, took up Corps Reserve line just beyond Village. Battn. returned to billets at 9.0 pm	
	30.3.18			
	31.3.18		At 12.30 am moved off & took over support line at HANGARD. Relieved advice of about 300 Reinforcements from 12th Wiltenbury Battn.	

T2134. Wt. W708—776. 500000. 4/15. Sir J.C. & S.

Army Form C. 2118.

WAR DIARY
or
INTELLIGENCE SUMMARY.
(Erase heading not required.)

Instructions regarding War Diaries and Intelligence Summaries are contained in F. S. Regs., Part II. and the Staff Manual respectively. Title pages will be prepared in manuscript.

Place	Date	Hour	Summary of Events and Information	Remarks and references to Appendices
			Officers joined during month	
			2/Lieut H.J. CHAPPMAN Joined 10.3.18	
			Capt. W.P. LOUSADA " "	
			2/Lieut F.G. NORAN " 18.3.18	
			2/Lieut S.H. WEBB (Rolled from 3rd R.W. Kent (T.F.) Joined 19.3.18	
			Lieut Col J.D. CROSTHWAITE M.C. Joined 10.3.18	
			Officers Casualties during month	
			Lt Col J.D. CROSTHWAITE M.C. Missing 21.3.18 . 2/Lt H.P. RIMINGTON Missing 24/3/18	
			Capt E. WYATT " " 2/Lt E.V. SAWYER Wounded & Missing "	
			" A. JOBLY " " 2/Lt J.A. FRENCH Missing "	
			Lieut P.B. WHITROW " " 2/Lt W.F. DRAIN " "	
			" B. VAUGHAN " " 2/Lt H.LYTH HATON " "	
			" A.A. EASON Wounded " 2/Lt E.A. THOMAS Wounded "	
			2/Lieut J.F. HEATLY Missing " 2/Lt H.T. RAPSON Missing "	
			" S.H. WEBB " " 2/Lt B.T. M. ELLIS " "	
			" G.M. HEATH " " 2/Lt W.U.C. TAYLER " "	

Army Form C. 2118.

WAR DIARY
or
INTELLIGENCE SUMMARY.
(Erase heading not required.)

Place	Date	Hour	Summary of Events and Information	Remarks and references to Appendices
			Officers’ Casualties during march (contd)	
			Capt. Revd G.R. COOKE. MC (C.F.) attached Missing 21.3.18	
			Capt. H.S. MOORE (R.A.M.C.) M.O. attached " "	
Field	2.5.18			
			J.A. Watson Lieut Col	
			COMDG. 7th BATTN. ROYAL WEST KENT REGT.	

A P P E N D I C E S

79, 80, 81 and 82 .

APP. 79 {WAR DIARY / COY No}

SECRET.

CIDER.
ORDER NO. 55.   6   Nov 3 1918

Ref Map
Sheet 66C
S.W. and N.W.
1/10,000.

1. There will be an entire Company relief on the night of the 6/7th Nov. 6.18.

2. "B" Coy will relieve "A" Coy in the front line (Mays & Vectis) & "A" Coy will move to Lavaron.
"D" Coy will move to our Support in Lavaron Line (Mays & Vectis).
"A" Coy will take the on Support.
"C" Coy will be in reserve.
The attached Diagram of "D" Coy area showing the location of Platoon of "B" Coy at FO/a 45

3. One guide per Platoon will be found by "A" and "B" Coys.
Guides of "A" Coy will be at the Somali Sphere Junction Crosses rendezvous at 1936.59 at 7.0 p.m. for the "B" Coy will be at the Draw road at M.9 b.9 from the Sunken Rd to be met by Guides of "A" to be located Platoon level to lead to the draw road at M.6 & J.3. to guide No. 6 Platoon "B" Coy to 45. Position on the right the Platoon will wait for the Platoon to front to be relieved & guide to front to be relieved Platoon back when to relief is completed, living the released on being will be arranged mutually between the Commanders of "A" and "D" Coys.

and moved to Belgium as A.A.
at 6:30 am to take up
Rations + been perfecting
Posns.
Rations, A Coy. out to
attached ration to C Coy H.Q.
and the remained from B.H.Q.
to dumps to fuw
Inspection Station M.D.
+ attended. Dr. Robson S.
Mykhael Cross

Leave at 11 a.m.
            6 Am Coy
Leaves No 1 Co.   J Sc.
       2 "
       3 B Coy
       4 C Coy
       5 D Coy

Following Equipments:-

A KNIFE   C SPOON
B FORK   D PLATE

8. On Alarm the Civilian &
R.O. of Watch-keeper and
2 medical orderlies the Canteen
assistant and 2 Police will
be attached to Bn Formation.

9. 1 N.C.O. from Station from A
and C Coys will report to
Batalion H.Q. at 6pm to
take over trench stores etc. &
for Bn Machine Coys. The
N.C.O's will return to their
Coys to act as Guides for
tack parties.

10. Cooks of B and D Coys and
report to the ICE FACTORY
at 6.30 p.m. to take over
kitchens
Cooks of A and C Coys.

4. 200 yds distance at ground
angle to from time of time again
claims. Machine guns taken for
fighting are not touched up where
found and are guarding.

5. All men to turn on trench
orders, photographs, etc
connected with each each
will be handed over on relay
Details of even on hand and
consolidated will ab. be
taken over.

6. Coy of Trench Stores taken from
15 Coys as a whole or by
detached posts and the Bn
to Battalion Orderly Room
as soon as possible after
relief

7. Coys send report relating
complete to ensuring the

SECRET.

BATTALION PROVISIONAL DEFENCE SCHEME.
BATTALION IN BRIGADE RESERVE.

Ref. maps
66 c N.W. 1/20,000
66.c.S.W.

10th March 1918.

1. Dispositions of the troops available for defence of the Bde sector on Battle Zone.

    (a) Normal disposition:-
        Battalion H.Q. and 2 Companies.   LY-FONTAINE.
        1 Company   RE MIGNY
        1 Company   CAPONNE FARM
        2 Coys Pioneers.   REMIGNY.
        H.Q. and 2 sect R.E. and Att.Inf.   —do—
        2 Sect. R.E. and Att. Inf.   H.28.d.
        1 Sect. Light T.M.Battery.   MOULIN FARM
    (b) Battle Dispositions:-
        See tracing "D" already issued to Companies.

2. Principles of Defence:
    (a) Organisation in depth of all arms.
    (b) The improvement of material defences and obstacles, and the careful use of ground in order to develop to the utmost the fire power of artillery and M.G's and so economise Infantry.
    (c) The maintenance of the fighting and energy and morale of the troops.
    (d) Activity and aggressiveness.
    Before the enemy attack developes to gain control completely of " NO MAN'S LAND" and so prevent surprise, and to raise the morale of the defence at the expense of that of the enemy.
    (e) After the attack develops _Counter attack.
    (g) Artillery Counter preparation.

3. Action in the event of an Attack:
    In the event of an attack or the probobility of attack, the following will be the procedure:-
    (1) The Message "Prepare for attack" will be sent out, on receipt of which all troops will get ready to move at 15 minutes notice to their Battle positions.
    (2) The message "Man battle positions" will be sent out, on receipt of which:-
    (a) All troops detailed for the defence of the battle zone will move into position.
    (b) Artillery will commence a regular and heavy bombardment of the enemy's front zone.
    (c) Units detailed for the defence of the battle zone will each detail one officer, the 2nd in command, to proceed to Bde H.Q. to act as Liaison officer: he will be accompanied by one runner.
Two days rations will be taken.

4. Units manning the battle zone will proceed in Fighting Order,170 rounds S.A.A. per man except those mentioned in S.S. 135 Sec (xxxl) 2 (VII).
Lewis Guns Teams will carry 24 drums.

5. Any Officer will carry out any of the instructions mentioned in para 3 without waiting for either of the two messages mentioned in 3 (I) and 3 (II); if in his opinion a situation arises which nesessitates such action.

6. Companies will report their arrival in position to Bn.H.Q. at the KEEP, LY FONTAINE.

O V E R.

7. All routes to battle positions will be reconnoitred and marked.
O.C.Coys. platoons and sections are responsible that all N.C.O's and men under their command know their battle position and the shortest way from their billets to them.

8. The company billeted at REMIGNY will be the Counter Attack Company. its battle position is in the Area N 8B
This Company will be ready to Counter-Attack immediately on the following places in the event of the enemy penetrating the Battle Zone at these places or between them:-
LY FONTAINE VILLAGE - N.15.a.5.9. - N.9.b.9.8. - N.4.a.4.2.
The Officer in command of this company will be prepared to Counter-attack on his own initiative without waiting for orders.
The guiding principle in deciding when the crucial moment for delivering the Counter-attack has arrived is; Never to Counter-attack until there is some definite enemy to Counter attack. The O.C. Counter attack Company must reconnoitre the ground and make his plans beforehand. He will discuss them and explain them to Platoon and Section Commanders All routes forward will be carefully reconnoitred and marked: Good positions for covering fire and observation post's noted and arrangements for communication made.
The O.C.Counter attack company will ensure that his company is well provided with wire cutters.

9. **Action in case of S.OS:**
Troops in the Battle Zone on seeing the S.O.S. or receiving a S.O.S message will adopt the state of readiness mentioned in para 3 (I)

10. **Role of Troops Garrisoning Battle Zone:**
Under no circumstances will the troops normally garrisoning the Battle Zone be moved forward to reinforce the FORWARD ZONE until they have been relieved by a similar number of troops and then only by order of Bde. H.Q.

11. **The Commander of the Bde Battle Zone Sector** will be the O.C. Inf Battalion holding that sector.
His Battle H.Q. will be the KEEP LY FONTAINE.

12. **The Regimental Police** will form posts at (1) N.2.c.4.9. (2) H.32.b.30
The Officer in charge Headquarter sections will ensure that they are acquainted with their posts.

13. **Ammunition Dumps, S.A. Bombs etc:**
Brigade Reserve Dump H.33.c.6.8. (Bde H.Q) Reserve Dumps have been formed at H.27.b.2.8., H.32.d.8.4. H.33.b.70.45., N.2.d.8.9., N.3.a.2.7., N.3.d.3.4., N.3.d.8.3., N.9.d.0.3.
These dumps are not to be used except in special cases.

14. **R.E.Dumps:**
Div. advanced dump at REMIGNY.

15. **Medical arrangements:**
Regimental aid post LY FONTAINE (N.3.d.0.5).
Advanced dressing station is at REMIGNY. (N.14.c.2.6).

Reference para 3 after sub para c. add:-
(d) The Signalling Officer will detail Signallers to man the relay station at N.9.b.15.55. as a transmitting station and will also send 3 signallers to Bde H.Q. to assist in manning the Brigade Visual Station.

16. ACKNOWLEDGE.

(Signed:-) H.T.RAPSON. Lieut.
Adjutant. CIDER.

S E C R E T.   Copy No........

7th Battalion Royal West Kent Regiment.
ORDER No. 89.

Ref. maps. Sheets   11th March 1918.
66c N.W. & S.W.
1/20,000.

1. The Battalion will be releived by the 10th Battalion ESSEX REGT on the night of the 12th/13th March 1918.

2. "B" Coy (left front line Coy) will be releived by "D" Coy of the ESSEX.
"D" Coy (right front line Coy) will be releived by "B" coy of the ESSEX.
"A" Coy (Support Coy) will be releived by "A" Coy of the ESSEX.
"C" Coy (Reserve Coy) will be releived by "C" Coy of the ESSEX.

3. 1 Guide for each platoon and 1 for Coy. H.Q. will be provided by each Coy.
   Each Guide will be furnished with a slip of paper stating for whom he is to act as guide and also the NAME of the post to which he is to guide his party.
   The post at H.30.d.0.4. will be known as "NEW POST".
   All guides from Coys will be at the X roads at H.30.c.55.35 at the following times :-

   "B" Coy   9.0 pm.   "A" Coy   11.15 pm.
   "D" "   9.30 pm.   "C" Coy.   11.15 pm.

4. After releif, Coys will move off independently to billets which are as follows:-
   "A", "B" (and Bn. HQ)   LY-FONTAINE.
   "C" Coy   CAPONNE FARM
   "D" Coy   REMIGNY.

5. All trench stores, dispositions etc, will be handed over to-morrow.
   For this purpose an advance party from the ESSEX will report at Bn.H.Q. at 4.30 am. where a guide will take them to "B" and "D" Coys.
   Advanced party for "A" and "C" Coys, will report to Bn.H.Q. at 3 pm. and will be sent to their respective Coys.

6. 16 Lewis Gun Magazines per Gun will be carried.
   The remaining 32 per Coy of "B" and "D" Coys together with box periscopes hedging gloves, bill hooks and Officers kits will be dumped at the ICE FACTORY by 7.30 pm. and will be taken charge of by L/C Mannering (Regtl. Police).   Here they will be loaded on to the Transport limbers when they arrive.
   The 32 Magazines, periscopes etc, of "C" Coy., and A.A. Guns and Magazines of H.Q. together with Signalling gear and officers kits ("C" and H.Q.), will be dumped at Bn.H.Q. to be loaded on the limbers under the supervision of the RSM.
   The 32 Magazines, periscopes etc. of "A" Coy together with officers kits will be dumped on the road near "A" Coy H.Q. to be loaded on to the limbers by 7.30 pm.
   As regards the above mentioned stores, great care should be taken to ensure that they are put on the limbers which are going to their respective Coys billets.

7. The Chaplain, his servant, the M.O., 2 stretcher bearers, 2 medical orderlies, canteen assistt and 2 police will proceed with "B" Coy.

8. Coys will report releif complete by wiring the following CODE words :-

           "A" SPRING   "C" AUTUMN
           "B" SUMMER   "D" WINTER.
   Coys will also report arrival in new billets to Bn. H.Q. at LY FONTAINE.
                                                              O V E R.

7th Battalion Royal West Kent Regiment. ORDER No: 89. (Continued)

Reference para 6:-
In addition to stores therein mentioned, steamers and dixies should be included, also Mess Gear.

Reference para 5 :-.
Range cards and tables for L.G's (diretion of fire) will also be handed over.

9. ACKNOWLEDGE.

           (Signed:-) H.T. RAPSON 2/Lieut
              Adjt. CIDER.

Issued at
Copies to:-
  No:1 C.O.
    2 "A" Coy
    3 "B" Coy
    4 "C" Coy
    5 "D" Coy.
    6 H.Q.
    7. R.S.M.
    8 War Diary
    9 File.

SECRET.   Copy No........

7th Battalion Royal West Kent Regiment.

ORDER No. 90.

APP. 83

18.3.18

Ref. maps:
Sheets. 66c
S.W. & N.W.
1/20,000

1. The Battalion will relieve the 10th Battalion ESSEX REGT. in the Southern sub-sector of the Northern sector of the 18th Divisional front on the night of the 19th/20th March 1918.

2. "A" and "C" Coys will be in the front line. ("A" on the left; "C" on the right); "D" in support and "B" in reserve.

3. 1-guide for each platoon and 1-for Coy Hd.Qrs of "A","B" and "D" Coys., and 1-for Battalion Hd.Qrs will be provided by the 10th Essex Regiment.
   These guides will be at MOULIN FARM as under:-
   "A" Co. 8.0 p.m.; "B" Co. 8.30 p.m.; "D" Co. 9.0 p.m.
   Battn. Hd.Qrs 9.30 p.m.
   1-guide for each platoon of "C" Coy., and 1-for Coy Hd.Qrs., will be at CAPONNE FARM at 8.0 p.m.
   200 yards distance will be maintained between platoons.

4. An advance party of 1-Officer, C.S.M., and 1-O.R per Coy., and 1-Officer from Hd.Qrs., will report at the Hd.Qrs of the 10th Essex Regt., at 2.0 pm. to take over Trench Stores, dispositions etc:
   In each case the Officer is to be in possession of Schedule in which is laid down the exact stores in the sector, and great care must be exercised in checking before taking over.

5. All maps, papers, defence schemes, photographs etc., connected with the sector will be handed over on relief. Details of work in hand and work contemplated will also be taken over.

6. 16-Lewis Gun Magazines per Coy., will be carried. In addition to this, 8-per Gun will be carried by Transport. They will be dumped with the rations of each Coy., and are to be drawn immediately on arrival.
   2-A.A.Guns with Magazines for Hd.Qrs will also be carried by Transport.
   The Reserve Coy will find guard for these Guns.

7. The following reports are required daily from Coys to reach Battn Hd.Qrs at the hours stated :-
   Situation Report————————3.30am. and 3.30 pm.
   Intelligence Report————————7.0am.)
   Patrol Report————————————7.0am.) For a period 6.0 am. to 6.9 a.m.
   Work Report—————————————7.0am.
   Trench Strength————————10.0 am.
   Marching-in and out State——10.0am.
   Casualty Return————————10.0am.
   Sick Report————————————10.0 am.

8. A Certificate that Trench Stores have been found correct, together with Trench Store List, will be forwarded to Battalion Hd.Qrs by 12.0 noon, 20th March 1918.

9. Coys will report relief complete by wiring the number of this order.

10. Rations for the two front line Coys will be brought up each night for the following day; and will be drawn as soon as possible after they arrive at the ICE FACTORY.
    Those for Support Coy will be dumped on main road near to Support Coy Hd.Qrs (H.36.b.2.5).

7th Battalion Royal West Kent Regiment.   ORDER No 90 (Continued).

10. (Contd). Those for Reserve Coy and Battn. Hd. Qrs will be dumped at Battn Hd.Qrs. (H.35.b.7.9.).

11. L/C. Mannering and 1-Regimental Policeman will remain on duty at the ICE FACTORY in charge of rations. These men will proceed with "C" Coy., and will be responsible for the dump each day.

12. 2-Cooks from "A" Coy will proceed with "C" Coy., and, with 2- from "C" Coy will cook for the two Coys at ICE FACTORY.
"D" and "B" Coys will make their own arrangements for cooking.
Meals will be as follows:-
    7.30 am.   Breakfast.
    12.30 pm.   Hot tea (Rations can be consumed at this hour).
    5.0 pm.   Dinner
    Midnight   Hot Tea.

13. All blankets will be rolled in bundles of 10-, tied in the middle and at each end, and clearly marked.
Those of "C" Coy., together with Officers Valises, will be stacked on the road at CAPONNE FARM by 6.30 pm., and will be taken away by a limber.
Those of "D" Coy will be stacked at Coy Hd.Qrs at REMIGNY by 6.0 pm to be called for by returning ration limbers.
Those of "A" and "B" and Hd.Qr Coys will be dumped at the CRUCIFIX at N.3.d.8.6. by 6.30 pm. and will also be called for by returning ration limbers.
In each case a runner will be left to look after blankets etc., until returning transport arrives. These men, when they have placed blankets and valises on the limbers, will proceed to Battn Hd.Qrs (H.35.b.7.9.) and there to join their coys.

14. All Officers Kits, Mess gear, hedging gloves etc., Lewis Gun magazines and signalling gear will be dumped with each Coys blankets and O's.C. Coys will make arrangements for them to be loaded on the limbers taking rations up to the line.
In the case of "C" Coy, the limber, before proceeding to the ICE FACTORY will call at CAPONNE FARM for these stores.

15. Canteen will proceed with "A" Coys Stores, and will be dumped at the ICE FACTORY.

16. Canteen assistant and 2-Police will be attached to "C" Coy for rations.

17. 2-Observers will report at Battn.Hd.Qrs. (H.35.b.7.9.) 10th ESSEX REGT., by 9.0 pm. to-night to take over O.P., and will remain in the line until the arrival of the Battalion.

18. REGIMENTAL AIDPOST will be at Battn. Hd.Qrs. (H.35.b.7.9.)

19. O's C Coys are responsible that all billets are left in a thoroughly clean and sanitary condition. A Certificate to this effect will be rendered to Battn. Orderly Room by 6.0pm. to-morrow

20. The Chaplain, his servant, the M.O. 2-stretcher bearers and 2-Medical Orderlies will be attached to Reserve Coy for accomodation and rations.

21. "Standing Orders for Companies when in the line", issued to Coys, 16/3/18, will be strictly adhered to.

22. ACKNOWLEDGE.

(Signed:-) H.T.RAPSON 2/Lt. Adj

Issued at..........pm.
Copy No:1......CO   Copy No5 O.C."B" Coy   Copy No 9 A/A
    2 2nd in Cmd   6 O.C."C" Coy   10 O.C 10th Essex Regt
    3 Q.M.   7 O.C "D" Coy.   11 T.O
    4 O.C. "A" Coy.   8 O.C Hd. Qrs   12 W. Diary

53rd Inf.Bde.
18th Div.

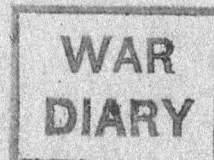

7th BATTN. THE ROYAL WEST KENT REGIMENT.

A P R I L

1 9 1 8

Attached:

Appendices 83, 84 & 85.

53/18
7th R West Kent Regt
April 1918

Army Form C. 2118.

WAR DIARY
or
INTELLIGENCE SUMMARY.
(Erase heading not required.)

Instructions regarding War Diaries and Intelligence Summaries are contained in F. S. Regs., Part II. and the Staff Manual respectively. Title pages will be prepared in manuscript.

Place	Date	Hour	Summary of Events and Information	Remarks and references to Appendices
GENTELLES	1.4.18		No. 12 Entrenching Battalion reorganised with remnants of 7th Bn R.W. Kent Regt. The whole to be called 7th Bn R.W. Kent Regt. Line reconnoitred E. of BOIS HANGARD. Relieve 10th Essex Regt in this sector; 3 Coys in front line, R.W. Kent Coy with 1 Yorkshire Regt, Yorkshire Regt in RESERVE on U.7.a.0.8.8. 8th E.Surrey Regt on left, 7th Bedford Regt on right.	APP. 83
	2.4.18		Quiet till known. Orders for line to be pushed forward to west running V.13 d.0.0 to copse at V.19.a.0.0. Attack carried out with partial success owing to heavy M.G. fire. New position consolidated 1 Carrier over by Reserve Coy	
	3.4.18		Heavy enemy T.M. barrage. Position improved. Reorganised. Dispositions altered to :- 2 Coys in front, 1 in support & 1 in Reserve.	
	4.4.18		Heavy T.M. barrage front. followed by enemy attack on Right about 5.30 am Coy 6.30 am enemy attacked left front Coy. Driven back by 2.6 & rifle fire. Artillery very active on both sides. At 3.0 pm enemy attacked left front Coy Driven back. Artillery casualties. At 5.0 pm enemy broke through Unit on left. Our line forced back to U.17.6 and c & incidentally established along road running N. and S. in U.17.a.c. Relieved by 10 Essex Regt at 11.0 pm & proceeded to GENTELLES. Champagne	
	5.4.18		reorganising. Line reconnoitred from U.7.a.0.0 to U.1.b.1.5.	

T2134. Wt. W708—776. 500000. 4/15. Sir J. C. & S.

Army Form C. 2118.

WAR DIARY
or
INTELLIGENCE SUMMARY.
(Erase heading not required.)

Instructions regarding War Diaries and Intelligence Summaries are contained in F. S. Regs., Part II. and the Staff Manual respectively. Title pages will be prepared in manuscript.

Place	Date	Hour	Summary of Events and Information	Remarks and references to Appendices
GENTELLES	6.4.18		Under command G.O.C. 1st Australian Inf. Bde. reconstituted CACHY switch line from U.13 cent. to U.13 cent.	
LINE	7.4.18		Relieved 10th Essex Regt in U.14 cent. in Counter attack Bn. at 8.0 pm. One coy march up to immediate support at 8.0 pm. to U.22 & 3.9. When withdrawal & reorganisation of Rgt's entire Australian Battns were complete, the coy withdrawn to U.21 a	
	8.4.18		Battn relieved by 10th Essex Regt at 8.0 am & proceeded to GENTELLES	
GENTELLES	9.4.18		Village heavily shelled. Battn moved to Trenches at about U.12 a. forward coy occupied position vacated by French counter attack Bn.	
LINE	10.4.18		Forward coy returned to U.12 a. at 3.0 pm. Battn relieved by 10th Essex Regt at 7.0 pm & proceeded to GENTELLES	
GENTELLES	11.4.18		Billets heavily shelled from 5.0 to 8.0 pm. Relieved 13th Essex Regt at U.14 cent. at 9.0 pm	
LINE	12.4.18		Heavy enemy attack on HANGARD & forward coy under 2nd R.M.F.O.T.G.R. Counter attacked at 10.0 am 70 am Reached West edge of square & dug in : 14 prisoners taken. NC. & artillery barrage prevented objective being completely gained. Touch established with Australian Bn. on left. Right flank secured at 11.0 am by remaining 3 coys. Touch maintained with French at U.28.b. Battn relieved at 9.30 p.m. by 18th Australian Battn. & proceeded to BOVES	
	13.4.18		Battn proceeded at 11.30 am. to ST FUSCIEN arriving at 1.30 pm	

Army Form C. 2118.

WAR DIARY
or
INTELLIGENCE SUMMARY.
(Erase heading not required.)

Instructions regarding War Diaries and Intelligence Summaries are contained in F. S. Regs., Part II. and the Staff Manual respectively. Title pages will be prepared in manuscript.

Place	Date	Hour	Summary of Events and Information	Remarks and references to Appendices
ST. FUSCIEN	14.4.18		Resting, re-organising & re-equipping. Divine Service. 160 Reinforcements arrived.	
	15.4.18		Training & Re-organising.	
	16.4.18		" " " Lt Col L. H. HICKSON assumed command vice Lt Col W. H. DIXON M.C.	
	17/19.4.18		" " "	
	20.4.18		" " " 86 Reinforcements arrived. Orders received to be in motor readiness to move.	
	21.4.18		Moved from ST. D. am 2nd Divine Service	
	22/23.4.18		Training & Re-organising	
	24.4.18		Battn. left St. 6.0 am. Stayed at BOVES till 11.0 am. Moved to S.32 Cent. (Sheet 62D SW) Bivouac	APP. 84
			By easy stages to Rue, arriving 9.30 pm. Counter attacked at 10.0 pm Objective gained but not held.	APP. 85
	25.4.18		Relieved at night in front of CACHY by Moroccan Division. Returned to new BOVES	
BOVES	26.4.18		Marched to SALEUX, arriving 9.0 pm	
SALEUX	27.4.18		Marched to CAVILLON. Start 7.30 am. arrived 3.0 pm	
CAVILLON	28.4.18		Relieved by 2nd Worcesters. Marched to METIGNY. Start 10.15 am. Arrival 4.0 pm	
METIGNY	29/30.4.18		Cleaning up & Re-organisation.	

T2134. Wt. W708—776. 500000. 4/15. Sir J. C. & S.

WAR DIARY or INTELLIGENCE SUMMARY

Army Form C. 2118.

(Erase heading not required.)

Place	Date	Hour	Summary of Events and Information	Remarks and references to Appendices
Scarpe Front			Officers Reinforcements during Month	
12th Infantry Brigade			Lt Col W. Hodson M.C. 2/Lieut J. Colin	
Battalion			Capt C.W.F. Dewdney " E.J. Salt	
	1.4.18		Major C. Player " T.F.R. Jones	
			Capt C. Edwards " C.W. Hill	
			" F. Lindsey-Jones " V.H. Bentley	
			" A. Hawkforth-Jones " W.E. Shepherd	
			" R.P. Bush " W.H. Dainton	
			2/Lieut A.V. Robinson " J. Humpage	
			" G.A. Cooke " W.H. Despres	
			" B.G. Thomson (16 R. Warks) " V. Walker	
			" F.G. Norris (16 R. Warks) " R. Love	
			" R. Ablett	
			Lieut L.H. Hicksey Rejoined 15.4.18	
			2/Lieut A.V.D. Morley M.C. Joined 14.4.18	
			2/Lieut J.O. Moody " "	
			" E.O. Aylett " "	
			" C.J. Tuck " 20.4.18	
			" S.H. Lewis " 23.4.18	
			Capt E.R. Smythe Rejoined	
			Lieut J.M. Harris M.C. "	
			" B. Bergh "	
			" N.V. Shepley-Green "	
			" D.V. Sutherst M.C. Rejoined	
			" D.G. Phipps "	
			" P. Stevens Joined	
			" H.W. Farley Rejoined	
			2/Lieut A.B. Gullerie	

Officers Casualties during Month

Lieut A.F.P. Jones Wounded 2.4.18
" A.V. Robinson " 4.4.18
Capt A.V. McDonald M.C. " "
2/Lt G.W.R. Dewdney Killed "
" F.J. Norris (W. Warks) " "
" V. Walker " "
" V.H. Bentley Missing "
" R. Ablett Wounded "
" H.H. Dainton " "
" R.H. Marsh Killed 12.4.18
" K. Blew " "
" J. Skottowe Wounded "
Capt C. Edwards " "
" R. Lovett " 24.4.18
2/Lieut E.O. Salt " "
" H.S. Chandley " "
" R. Wixleton-Bates " "
" J.O. Moody " "
Lieut H.W. Farley Wounded + Missing "
T/Lt D. Simpson Wounded Boarded T/S 12.4.18
" C.D. Tibbutt " to England 5.4.18
Capt E.N. Holt " " 22.3.18

A.E. Phipps Major
COMDG. 7th BATTL. ROYAL WEST KENT REGT.

APPENDICES

83, 84 and 85.

APP. 23

7th Batth. Royal West Kent Regiment.

NARRATIVE OF OPERATIONS. 1/22 April 1918

Ref. Map. Sheet 62d.

1-4-18. Lieut.Col. W.HODSON.M.C., Commanding 12th Entrenching Battn reported to 53rd. Infantry Brigade at 9.30 a.m., who ordered re-organisation of this Battn., together with a Coy of 7th R.W.Kent Regt., the whole to be called the 7th. R.W.Kent Rgt.

During the afternoon the line East of BOIS de HANGARD was reconnoitred and the Battn less the R.W.Kent Coy relieved 10th Essex Rgt in this sector the same night.
Dispositions. 3- Coys in front line, each finding their own supports and 1- Platoon composed of Cheshires attached to the R.W.Kent Coy in reserve at U.22.a.8.8.
8th E.Surreys on left and 7th Bedfords on left right.

2-4-18. Quiet night and forenoon. Received orders during the afternoon that in conjunction with the 54th Inf. Bde., 7th.R.W.Kents were to engage in an operation which had as its objective the pushing forward of our line to the crest running from V.13.Cent. to the Copse at V.19.a.8. 4.

7th Bedfords were ordered to proceed along the right and reach the Copse from the rear. On arriving at this copse to fire a succession of white Very Lights as a signal for 7th R.W.Kents to assault.

The movement of the 7th Bedfords was to be covered by L.G. and rifle fire from a position which had to be taken up by the left Coy of the 7th R.W.Kent Rgt as near V.13.Cent. as possible. This movement by the left Coy was observed by the enemy and some casualties were incurred in reaching this position.

One Coy was detailed for the assault with another Coy supporting it.

The assaulting Coy assembled along Bank in U.18.d.33. to U.24.b.3.6.

The 7th Bedfords failed to reach the Copse and did not put up the signal, but the look-out man posted up a tree mistook a string of enemy white lights put up from near the Copse at 7.40 p.m., for the pre-arranged signal, and the assaulting waves went over. They were met by heavy machine gun fire, but persisted in their advance until reaching a copse - not marked on the map - which they mistook for their objective. Here they remained and dug-in.

Our right flank being exposed, two platoons detailed beforehand for the purpose formed a defensive flank linking up with the unit on the right. Re-organised during the night. The R.W.Kent Coy who had come up during the evening took over the line held by the attacking Coy., who withdrew as Reserve Coy.

3-4-18. At dawn, enemy seen on our left engaged in work on their trench, and dispersed with rifle fire.

Heavy enemy T.M.barrage in front of wood in U.18.d., and V.13.a during afternoon and evening.

During the night we improved existing posts and dug a fresh dog-leg trench from U.18.c. 4.9. to U.18.c.6.9. and from U.18.c.6.9. to U.18.c.8.4.; also dug a trench from U.18.c.3.9. to U.17.d.9.3.

2.

3-4-18. (Contd.) Dispositions altered during the night; 2- Coys in front line, 1- Coy in support and 1- in reserve at U.17.d., less 1- platoon U.22.a.

4-4-18. At 5.0 a.m. heavy T.M. barrage all along our front, followed by an enemy attack on the unit on our right.
At 6.30 a.m. enemy attacked left front Coy at about V.13.Cent., but was driven back to his trenches by L.G. and rifle fire.
Artillery active on both sides throughout day, and enemy heavy T.M. falling all along our front.
At 3.0 p.m. enemy again attacked left front Coy and were again driven back to their original positions, suffering heavy casualties.
About 5.0 p.m. enemy broke through unit on our left and came round N.E. edge of wood in V.7.c., working through the wood and attempting to cut off our front line.
Telephone communication between Battn.H.Q. and front line broken.
Our line held out until their ammunition was expended, and narrowly escaped being cut off altogether.
The reserve Coy were formed up along the line running W. and E. in U.17.d. and U.18.e.
The enemy at length broke through the S.W. edge of wood in U.18.d and to meet this the reserve Coy took up a line running N. and S. along the front of BOIS de HANGARD in U.18.a. and c.
The enemy now opened with intense M.G.fire from N.W. edge of wood in U.12.d and U.18.a and caused heavy casualties
Aided by this M.G.fire our line was forced back through the wood in U.17.b and d. and eventually our line was established along the road running N. and S. in U.17.a. and c.
It was now getting dark and the attack not being pressed further, re-organisation was proceeded with, and touch established with units on right and left, being maintained throughout the night by patrols.

5-4-18. Relieved by 10th ESSEX Rgt. at 5.0 a.m. and proceeded to GENTELLES.
After relief by 10th ESSEX RGT.,
Cleaning up and re-organising. Reconnoitred line from U.7.a.40. to 7.1.b.1.5.

6-4-18. Under Command G.O.C. 5th Australian Inf.Bde., reconnoitred CACHY switch line from U.13.Cent to U.3.Cent.

7-4-18. Relieved 10th ESSEX RGT. in U.14.Cent as Counter Attack Battn., at 20 a.m.
Australian (Right and Centre Battns.) attacked BOIS de HANGARD at 5.0 a.m. After capturing objectives they had to withdraw to original positions at 8.0 p.m. I moved up one Coy to U.22.b.3.9. as immediate support while withdrawal and re-organisation of Australians in progress. Passed without incident and Coy withdrawn to U.21.a

8-4-18. Relieved by 10th ESSEX RGT at 8.0 a.m. and handed over dispositions as under :-
1- Coy at U.21.a., and 3- Coys and H.Q. at U.14.Cent.
Proceeded to GENTELLES.

9-4-18.
Village heavily shelled and Coys moved out to trenches at about U.12.a. At 4.30 p.m. received orders from 5th Australian Inf. Bde. to move into position as counter attack Battn at once, as information received of impending enemy attack on HANGARD.

Visited French Counter attack Bn. Hd.Qrs and arranged concerted action as follows :-
- (a) If a break through by enemy is localised as limited to French sector, the French Counter attack Battn located at U.21.d.16 countered and my forward Coy moved to the position vacated by the French at U.21.d.1.6 with a Platoon extended along valley from about U.27.b.2.4 to U.27.d.5.5.
- (b) If the break occurred on our own sector we countered, keeping French closely informed and acting in concert with O.C. Right Australian Battn.
- (c) If the break occurred on a wide front, the counter attack to take place in conjunction with French counter attack Battn; my Right flank to take in Copse at U.22.c.5.0. inclusive.

To maintain liason I left a French speaking Officer with Left flank of Counter Attack Battn at U.21.d.1.6.

While I was at French H.Q., the bombardment of HANGARD broke out, and at 7.0 p.m the enemy attacked and captured part of HANGARD. French Counter Attack Battn launched impetuous counter attack in the dark and restored the situation. My forward Coy moved to position vacated by French, Counter Attack Bn., but were rather late as French Counter Attack Bn moved away without letting either me or O.C. Right Australian Bn know they were going.

10-4-18.
On return of French my Coy returned to U.21.a at about 3.0 a.m. Day passed without incident. Relieved by 10th ESSEX RGT at 7.0 p.m. and proceeded to GENTELLES.

11-4-18.
GENTELLES heavily shelled from 5.0 p.m. to 8.0 p.m. Relieved 10th ESSEX RGT in U.14.Cent. at 9.0 p.m.

Carried 300 Stokes Mortars into HANGARD, party returning at 1.0 a.m. 12th.

12-4-18.
At 7.0 a.m. a strong enemy attack on HANGARD and Copse at U.29.a. began. I moved to Australian H.Q., keeping in touch with O.C. Enemy attack progressing, HANGARD being captured also Copse at U.29.a. At 10.0 a.m. was ordered to counter attack Copse at U.29.a. with forward Coy as Right flank was threatened. This Coy under 2/Lieut. R.P.WOODYEAR succeeded in reaching Western edge of copse and capturing a few prisoners, but were not strong enough, owing to their being caught in a heavy M.G. and artillery barrage, to go through the copse. They dug-in 40 yds from Western edge of copse, and linking up with Australians on their Left, maintained this position throughout the day. Right flank situation not clear. Remaining 3 Coys had meanwhile moved forward and were ordered to take up position to cover right flank. This was accomplished, the right extending into valley at U.28.b where touché was maintained with French.

12-4-18
(Contd.) The 10th ESSEX RGT. counter attacked at 7.30 p.m. in conjunction with the French and restored the situation.

Battalion relieved at 9.30 p.m. by 18th Australian Battn., and proceeded to BOVES.

(Signed:-) W. HODSON. Lieut.Col.
Commdg., 7th Battn. Royal West Kent Regiment.

Field.
16-4-18.

7th Batt Royal West Kent Regt. A.F. 84 Copy No 1.

SECRET
Ref Sheet 62.D
1/40,000

OPERATION ORDER No 2

W.D.

APRIL 23rd/1918.

1. **INFORMATION.** It seems probable that the enemy will attack on the AMIENS front on 'A' day

2. **INTENTIONS.** 3RD CORPS will hold VILLERS-BRETONNEUX PLATEAU as Battle position at all costs.
    58TH DIV will hold RIGHT DIV front
    8TH " " " LEFT " "
    18TH " in RESERVE
    The 54th Bgde will be held for Counter Attack on the RIGHT DIV front.
    The 53rd Bgde will be held for Counter Attack on the LEFT DIV front and the recapture of VILLERS BRETONNEUX.

3. **STATE OF READINESS.**
    Battalion will be in a state of immediate readiness from now.
    On development of attack, the order to "STAND TO" will be given & BATT will be in readiness to move at 15 mins notice

4. ORDERS TO COMPANIES.
   Coys will each send a Runner to Batt. HQ at 8.0 PM or on receipt of Warning Order.
   On receipt of order "STAND TO" Companies will fall in in Fighting Order on Coy Parade Ground and will await orders to move.
   Coy Lewis Gun O.S. limbers will at once be loaded.

5. ORDER of MARCH
   H Q Coy. A.B.C.D + TRANSPORT as allotted as follows
   (a) To accompany Batt.
      4 Lewis Gun limbers
      1 T.M. limber.
      1 S.A.A. limber
      1 Spare S.A.A. limber which will return to Transport Lines after unloading
   (b) To remain at T.L. a 6.6.
      2 S.A.A. limbers.
      2 Cookers
      1 Water Cart.
      1 Mess Cart.
      Pack animals

(5).

    (c) To remain at ST. FUSCIEN.
          1 Limber
          2 Cookers
          1 Water Cart.
          Maltese Cart

'Z' hour will be notified later. Bgd HQ will pass starting point at Z plus 10 min.

On order to move head of HQ Coy will pass S.13.b.9.8 on BOVES Rd at Z plus 15.

1st Stage S.13.b.9.8 by BOVES ROAD to S.6.d
2nd Stage. S.6.d by bridge near AYRE at S6.a.8.8. under Railway Bridge at T.1.a.6.3. to N.27.a.&c.

Units will avoid all ground under observation of Enemy.

Platoons will move at 100 yds interval

6. Bgd HQ will be at N.27.a.&c immediately South of road.

On arrival of Batt at N.27.a.&b 2nd in command + 1 mounted orderly + 2 runners will report at Bgd HQ

Transport & Baggage will move under TO + QM as ordered by Bgd HQ

7. All Kits will be collected at Billets under arrangements by QM.

Issued at 11.30 pm.

J W Stenning
2nd Lieut
a/Adjt.
7th Batt Royal West Kent Regt.

Copies to. C.O.
2nd in Command.
HQ
A. Coy
B. "
C. "
D. "
TO.
QM.
Diary.

W.D APP 85

7th Battalion Royal West Kent Regiment

5th Infantry Brigade

OPERATIONS — April 24th & 25th 1918

Ref Map
Sheet 62D 1/40,000

1. At 7.30 pm April 24th, 7th Battn Royal West Kent Regt was placed under orders O.C. 5th Infantry Brigade to take part in counter-attack in lieu of 11th Battn Royal Fusiliers, and Battalion was concentrated at U.6.c Central by 8.0 pm.

2. Orders — Forming up line U.3.g.15 all Central
   Zero hour 10.0 pm
   Final Objective — Northern boundary — U.17.d.0.2
   Southern boundary — U.17.a.4.8
   Flank of attack — 9th London Regt on RIGHT flank
   1st Bedford Regt on LEFT flank

Plan of attack — 'C' and 'A' Coys (less
2 Coy) in RESERVE
Attack was to pass through 58th
Division and carry their troops forward

Artillery.
A Standing Barrage Each
on U.A.16 central till Z + 30
and left to final objective till
Z + 60.
Protective Barrage to left
300× East of final objective and
stand for ½ hour.

3. Dispositions
'A' and 'B' Coys — 1st Wave
'C' and 'D' Coys — 2nd Wave
Battn Hd Qrs established at U.15.a
10.7

4. Narrative
At 8.30 am Battalion moved
by Companies from U.6.c central
by SENTELLES–CACHY Road to
CACHY–DOMART Road.
At 10.0 pm 'A' and 'B' Coys
were in position to East of Road
but 'C' and 'D' Coys were not in

4. Narrative
(cont.) position till 10.0 and 10.15 pm respectively.

On the Left, touch had not been established with 7th Bedfords, but this was gained by 'B' Coy during their advance. On the Right, time did not allow of getting into touch with left flank of 9th Gordons.

As it was uncertain whether 9th Gordons were in position, 'D' Coy was held in Reserve on its arrival, to cope with possible counter attack from BOIS HANGARD, and one company 6th Northants placed at disposal by O.C. 6th Northants, was used for 2nd Wave.

At 10.5 pm 'A' and 'B' Companies advanced.

'A' and 'B' Coy and part of 'C' Coy reached final objective and were approximate to it, but owing to heavy losses, mostly from machine gun fire, were unable to retain, and fell back to line U.10.b.2.3 - U.15.b.9.8. which was held throughout April 25th 'D' Coy reinforced.

'B' Coy had heaviest casualties and this caused a gap between the Battalion and 7th Bedfords

4.

Narrative (cont'd)

enemy withdrawal from objective.

Communication was opened with 9th Londons along CROIX - DUPART Road, and their advance into HAVRINCOURT WOOD was reported to progress, but right flank of N/Hants Regiment was unable to join up with them, though patrol during the night got into touch.

During early morning April 25th. enemy pushed patrols forward in gap under cover of mist and established M.G. Post in U.10.b. which impeded patrols attempting to get touch with right flank of Bedfords Regt.

Enemy were consolidating in line U.3-11.17 central during morning, and considerable movement was seen. At 3.0 pm artillery fire was opened on them and good results appeared to be obtained.

At 6.15 pm enemy appeared to be organising attack, and put an intense bombardment on U.3.9.15 and back areas for 1 hour. Protective barrage was opened.

5.

4. Narrative (cont)

A part of the enemy reached a point near our front line, but the attack was not pressed.

At 1.0 am 26th April the Battalion was relieved by a Moroccan Division.

5. Strength of Battalion going into action
17 Officers
481 Other Ranks

Casualties:-
Officers:- Wounded - Capt. F.C.LOVETT
Wdd & Missing - Lt. H.V.L.FARLEY
-do- 2/Lt. J.O.MOODY
Wounded - 2/Lt. E.O.SALT
-do- 2/Lt. R.SINGLETON-GATES
-do- 2/Lt. H.G.CHANDLER

Other Ranks - Killed 14)
Wdd. 85)
Wdd & M. 1) 228
Missing 128)

Field.
30/4/18

Lieut. Col.

Army Form C. 2118.

WAR DIARY
or
INTELLIGENCE SUMMARY. 7th BATTN. ROYAL WEST KENT REGT.

(Erase heading not required.)

Instructions regarding War Diaries and Intelligence Summaries are contained in F.S. Regs., Part II. and the Staff Manual respectively. Title pages will be prepared in manuscript.

Place	Date	Hour	Summary of Events and Information	Remarks and references to Appendices
METIGNY.	1/2-5-18.		Battalion in billets. Cleaning up and reorganisation. Special training of Lewis Gunners, Signallers and Scouts.	
	3-5-18.		Ceremonial Parade and Presentation of Ribbons by Corps Commander.	App. 86.
	4-5-18.		Training. Warning Order to move on 5th.	App. 87.
	5-5-18.		Battalion proceeded by Lorries to MONTIGNY. Parade 8.15a.m. Embussed 11.0a.m. Arrived 5.0p.m. Transport by March route. Battle surplus marched to Reinforcement Camp.	
MONTIGNY.	6-5-18.		"C" Company attached 8th. Battn. Royal Buffs Regt., to relieve 1 Company 19th. London Regt. in BAIZIEUX line at D.7.a. Rest of Battalion ordered to take over billets at BEHENCOURT.	App. 88.
	7-5-18.		Move postponed till 7th. Battalion (less "C" Coy.) moved to BEHENCOURT 9.30a.m., arriving 9.45 a.m. Provisional Order to move to 1st. Assembly Position at C.14.a on receipt of Alarm.	
BEHENCOURT.	8-5-18.		Battalion moved at 6.0a.m. to 2nd. Assembly Position at C.18.d. in reserve for Counter Attack. Arrived 7.50a.m. At 10.30 p.m., relieved 8th. Battn. East Surrey Regt., in Left Sub Sector, Right Brigade front.	App. 89. App. 90-91.
LINE.	9-5-18.		Battalion in Line. Work on Dug-outs and improvement of trenches.	
	10-5-18.		" " " Slits dug 50 yards in front of existing front and support trenches as protection from T.M. Fire. Desultory Gas Shelling.	
	11/12-5-18.		-do- -do- -do-	
	13-5-18.		-do- Improvements to PIP STREET and new communication trenches.	App. 92.
	14-5-18.		Battalion relieved by 10th. Battalion Essex Regt.; Relief complete 12.0 midnight. Moved to Counter Attack position arriving about 2.0a.m. Disposition:— 2 Coys. DARWIN SUPPORT. D.17.a.	App. 93.
			1 Coy. LAVIEVILLE TR. D.16.c & a.	
			1 Coy. Shelters. D.21.b.	
			Bn. H.Q. D.21.b.51.	
	15-5-18.		Battalion in Counter Attack position. -- Work on building and improvement of Dug-outs.	
	16-5-18.		-do- -do- -do-	
	17-5-18.		"A" and "B" Coys. relieved by 11th. Battn. Fusiliers. Battalion detailed to hold LAVIEVILLE LINE under 54th. Brigade.	App. 94-95. App. 96.
	18-5-18.		Working Parties on Trenches and Strong Points under Div. R.E.	App. 97.
	19-5-18.		Battalion moved into Reserve Area at about c.18.d.24.	
	20-5-18.		Battalion in Reserve. Company Inspections.	
	21-5-18.		Battalion relieved 7th. Battn. Queens Regt., on left Battalion front, left Brigade Sector.	App. 98-99.
	22-5-18.		Battalion holding line.	
	23-5-18.		Battalion relieved by 19th. London Regiment. Moved to billets at WAPLOY.	App. 100.

Army Form C. 2118.

WAR DIARY
or
INTELLIGENCE SUMMARY.
(Erase heading not required.)

Instructions regarding War Diaries and Intelligence Summaries are contained in F.S. Regs., Part II. and the Staff Manual respectively. Title pages will be prepared in manuscript.

Place	Date	Hour	Summary of Events and Information	Remarks and references to Appendices
WARLOY.	24-5-18.		Cleaning up and Inspections.	
	25-5-18.		Battalion moved to camp in U.28.c. (Brigade in Corps Reserve for Counter Attack).	App. 100.a. " 100.b.
Near CONTAY.	26-5-18.		Company Inspections. Battle Surplus and 147 O.R. Reinforcements joined.	
	27-5-18.		Company inspections and training. Specialist training.	
	28/30-5-18.		Battalion burying Cable under R.E's. Specialist training.	
	31-5-18.		Reorganising and training. Specialist classes.	
			-do- -do- Warning Order recieved for relief, night of 1/2nd.	App. 101.
			Baths at VADENCOURT.	

OFFICERS JOINED DURING THE MONTH.

Capt. L.F.S. SPALDING. Joined. 1-5-18.
Major A.E.S. NORTHCOTE. " 15-5-18.
Capt. R. MALTBY. M.C. " 25-5-18.
2/Lt. P.D. GAUSDEN. Rejoined. 25-5-18.
2/Lt. C.R. ADDISON. " 25-5-18.

OFFICERS' CASUALTIES DURING THE MONTH.

2/Lieut. G.A. COCKS. Sick to England. 20-4-18.
Capt. W.P. LOUSADA. " " " 16-3-18.
Capt. T.T. WADDINGTON. M.C. To estab. of 4th. Army Inf. School from 29-12-17.
Lieut. R.P. BUSH. M.C. Sick to England. 24-5-18.
2/Lt. L.P. SOLOMONS. " " " 23-5-18.
Lieut. E.P. SMYTH. To 1st. Battn. Royal West Kent Regt. 1-5-18.
2/Lt. H.G.J. HINES. " " " " " " " 1-5-18.
2/Lt. W.E. SHEPHERD. " " " " " " " 1-5-18.
2/Lt. E.O.E. AYLETT. " " " " " " " 1-5-18.
2/Lt. C.J. TUCK. " " " " " " " 1-5-18.
Lieut. D.V. SUTHERST. M.C. To 53rd. T.M.B. 2-5-18.
Capt. S.H. LEWIS. To 23rd. Army Corps. BRENTWOOD. 3-5-18.
2/Lt. P.D. BERTRAM. To 53rd. T.M.B. 16-5-18.

Army Form C. 2118.

WAR DIARY
or
INTELLIGENCE SUMMARY.
(Erase heading not required.)

Instructions regarding War Diaries and Intelligence Summaries are contained in F.S. Regs., Part II. and the Staff Manual respectively. Title pages will be prepared in manuscript.

Place	Date	Hour	Summary of Events and Information	Remarks and references to Appendices
			HONOURS & AWARDS.	
	D.S.O.	-----	A/Lt. Col. W. HODSON M.C., Cheshire Regt., attached 7th. Battn. Royal West Kent Regt.,	
	M.C.	-----	T/Lieut. R.P. BUSH.	
			T/2/Lt. R.P. WOODYEAR. Cheshire Regt., attached 7th. Battn. Royal West Kent Regt.,	
			Lt. (A/Capt.) F.C. LOVETT. Royal West Kent Regiment.	
			Lt. H.E. FOSTER. M.O.R.C. Royal West Kent Regiment.	
			U.S.A. Med. Officer attached.	
			2/Lt. W.J. GODDARD.	
	D.C.M.	-----	25488. Sgt. Hughes.J.	
			470. L/C (A/Sgt. Tomkins.C. "H.Q." (since a casualty)	
			1575. C,S.M./A.R.S.M. Roffey.A.T. "H.Q." (since a Casualty).	
			2240. Sgt. Foot. W. "B" Company.	
	BAR TO MILITARY MEDAL.			
			1635. L/C. Rough. J.T. (M.M.) "H.Q." Company.	
			10421. Pte. Stacey. J. (M.M.) "H.Q." Company.	
			21329. L/C. Walker. G. (M.M.) "A" Company.	
	M.M.	-----	21683. L/C. Souls. A.W. - - - - - - (since a casualty.)	
			24830. Sgt. Elliot.A. - - - - - - (since a casualty.)	
			20718. Pte. Jilkes.W. "C" Coy.	
			5210. Cpl. Adkin. S.L.V. "H.Q." Coy.	
			202243 Pte. Stoney. W. "A" Coy.	
			290472. Pte. Wright. J.H. "A" Coy.	
			219214 Pte. Macnamara. F. - - - - - - (since a casualty.)	
			7804. Pte. Long. J. "B" Coy.	
			242253. Grimmett. H. "D" Coy.	
			21396. Pte. Turnell. G.B. "B" Coy.	
			38759. Pte. Phillips. A. "D" Coy.	
			13447. Sgt. Goulden. R.E. (D.C.M.) "C" Coy.	
			M.M.	
			32114. Pte. Hewitt. B.	"D" Coy.
			26954. Pte. Branagan. A.G.	"H.Q." "
			308. L/Sgt. Stevens. N.	
			51735. Pte. Williams. S.A.	

[signature]

LIEUT. COLONEL.
Commanding 7th. Battn. Royal West Kent Regiment.

SECRET   COPY No. 10

7th Battn Royal West Kent Regt.   APP. 86

ORDER No. 4

Map Ref   4th May 1918.

1. The Battn will proceed to the embussing point at H.20.c.6.9 (Fork Road, S.E. of WARLOG) on 5th inst.

2. Order of March   H.Q. A.B.C.D. Coys. The head of H.Q. Coy to pass junction of LALEU - AIRAINES Road at 8-15 a.m.

3. Dress:- Fighting Order. Blankets to be carried in packs.

4. Lieut Bergl and 1 Guide (from Q.M. Stores) will be at WARLUS church at 7-50 a.m. One Lorry will proceed from WARLUS to Battn Q.M. Stores at METIGNY will guide. Q.M. will arrange for Kits to be loaded
   (a) With Battn Kit.
   (b) With Stores etc for DADOS

Stores for DADOS will be dumped at CAVILLON. Battn baggage will proceed to X Road BEAUCOURT-MONTIGNY near Battn Dump.

                (Sd) W.A. SHEARING 2/Lt
                      7th Bn Royal West Kent Regt. a/Adjt

Issued at 11-45 p.m.

Copy No.		Copy No.	
1	C.O.	5	O.C. D Coy.
2	2nd in Command	6	Q.M.
3	O.C. A Coy	7	R.S.M.
4	O.C. B Coy	8	F.L.E.
		9	
		10 & 11	To Spare

SECRET   7th Bn Royal West Kent Regt   APR 87 No. 6

               Order No 5   6 May 1917

Map Ref
Sheet 62 D NW.

1. The 7th Bn R.W. Kent Regt (less C Coy) will move to BEHENCOURT today and will take over billets occupied by 8th Bn R Berks Regt

2. C Coy will be attached to 8th Bn R. Berks Regt and will report to OC 8th Bn R Berks Regt at 2.0 pm today at BEHENCOURT
C Coy Cookers & L.G. limber will move with the coy

3. Shops, Canteen Orderly Room Boxes, Signalling Gear & QM Stores will be loaded by 2.0 pm
Valises of Coy officers will be carried on Coy L.G. limbers
HQ valises will be dumped outside Bn HQ at 2.0 pm

4. Order of March
       H.Q. Coy
       D   "
       A   "
       B   "

-2-

6. The S.O.S Signal will be a Rifle Grenade bursting into 3 white stars, one over the other.
In the event of fog, this signal will be supplemented by whistles. The Battn on right will use bugles.
The ALARM will be given by 1 G if the attack is on front of the Right Bn. of the Brigade i.e. 8th R. Berks.
2 G's if on Left Battn Front i.e. 4th R.W. Kent.
3 G's if on whole Brigade Front.
(Note:- The supply of S.O.S. Signals is very limited and will be entrusted only to officers)

7. Completion of Relief will be reported to Battn HQ by Code words as under.

    "A" Coy.   BUSH
    "B" "   WOOD
    "C" "   GREEN
    "D" "   STEVE

Time of relief to be stated

8. There will be no cooking - no movement by day.
Hot Meals will be served at 2.30 am & 9.0 pm.

9. Companies will Stand-To at 2.30 am each morning until order to stand down is received from Battn H.Q.

ACKNOWLEDGE.

2 Lieutenant
a/adjutant
Issued at.   7th R.W. Kent Regt.

by No: 1 to.   C.O
       2   Adjutant
       3   H.Q.
       4   O.C. A Coy
       5   "   B "
       6   "   C "
       7   "   D "
       8   8th Bn E Surrey Regt.
       9   War Diary
      10   FILE.

SECRET.
7th Battn. R.W. Kent.
Defence Scheme.

APP 91

1. In the event of Enemy Offensive the line of resistance is the present front line which will be held to the last and a series of Counter Attacks made until the front line is re-established.

2. According to intelligence the enemy offensive should be expected any day within the next nine days.

The extensive use of Mustard Gas by the enemy should place all especially on the alert.

3. Plan: (a) 2 Lewis Gun posts, 1 found by Right Front Coy, and 1 by Left Front Coy, have been dug in "No Mans Land" about 120 yards on enemy side of our Front Line. These guns are intended to hamper & break up enemy forming for attack on the dead ground before us.

Lewis Gunners manning them should understand that the greatest value to security is our Front Line and post of great responsibility.

(b) Four standing patrol posts are established about 50 yards in front of our line and are manned by tours of 24 hours to watch dead ground where enemy may approach unseen.

(c) Right Front Coy. "C" Coy, 2 platoons

2

has 1 section in Front line, 1 section in support.

Left Front Coy "D" Coy, 2 Platoons in Front line, 1 Platoon in Support.

Role of Front Platoons is to hold Front line to the last.

Role of Support Platoon both fronts, to Counter attack immediately the enemy gain any footing in Front line of their respective Companies.

(d) Counter attack Coy. "A" Coy will counter attack immediately on enemy gaining footing in our Front line, on the initiative of their Company Commander, without awaiting orders from Battn. H.Q.

Immediately on Enemy attack O.C. Counter Attack Coy should send forward patrol to inform him of the situation. Separate orders will be issued to this officer as to method of Counter attack.

(e) Reserve Coy. "B" Coy, will be held under orders of O.C. Battn., 2 platoons in D.18.c. and 1 platoon at D.17.b.

Probable role to move to position of Counter attack Coy when the latter moves up to counter attack.

3/ 10th Essex Regt is in Reserve at about D.15.d as Counter attack Battalion on Bde Front.

3

8th Royal Berks are on our Right Flank with Battn H.Q at D.24.a.1.7 and 6th Northamptons on our Left Flank with Bn H.Q at D.12.d.9.9. Right and Left Front Companies are responsible for keeping liaison with neighbouring Company Commanders of these units and linking posts will be established in each case.

4/ 55th Inf. Bde is in Reserve at for purpose of Counter Attack on Divisional Front.

5/ Details of T.M.B, M.G.C and Artillery S.O.S. Barrage will be notified later.

6/ S.O.S. Bugle Posts are established as follows:-
   1- at Right Front Coy.
   2 with Battalion H.Q.
On S O S signal, bugler will sound the alarm followed by
   1 "G" if on Right Front Bn
   2 Gs if on Left Front Bn
   3 Gs if on whole Bde Front.
All Buglers will immediately repeat these calls when heard sounding on other Battalion Fronts. The object is to warn all ranks of an attack in

in fog or mist, where the S.O.S has sometimes failed to warn all units.

7. Battalion Command post will be at D.17.b.a.3.

8. These orders are to be committed to memory notes taken and then destroyed.

9. Special Points. DERNANCOURT- QUARRY- MILLEMCOURT ROADS. should be specially watched as likely points of attack.

SECRET
7th Battalion R.W. Kent Regt   Copy No 12
Operation Order No 9   **APP. 92**

Map. Ref.   14th May 1918.
Sheet 62 d N.E.

1. The 7th Battalion R.W. Kent Regt will be relieved on the night of the 14th/15th May 1918 by the 10th Battn Essex Regt.

2. Guides as under will report to Battn H.Q at 8 pm.
   <u>"A" Coy</u>   1 Guide for platoon in EMMA TRENCH
          1 Guide for platoon in COOKHOUSE ROAD
          1 Guide for Company H.Q
   To report to "A" Coy CIRCLE

   <u>"B" Coy</u>   1 Guide for platoon in COOKHOUSE ROAD.
          1 Guide for platoon in DOPIE DITCH
          1 Guide for Company H.Q.
   To report to "D" Coy CIRCLE.

   "C" Coy   1 Guide per platoon, 1 for Coy H.Q and 1 for Lewis Gun teams to report to "B" Coy CIRCLE

   "D" Coy.   2 Guides for front line, 1 for Lewis Gun teams & 1 for Coy H.Q. to report to "C" Coy CIRCLE.

   <u>Battn H.Q.</u>   1 Guide.

-2-

3. All maps, documents, French Stores, Aeroplane photos etc will be handed over to incoming unit. Receipts for same will be sent to Orderly Room by 9 AM on the 16th inst

Lewis Gun teams will hand over present positions, but will take away all mountings.

4. One limber will report to cookhouse at 9.30 p.m. to collect dixies of 'C' & 'D' Coys and all spare petrol tins other than those taken over from the East Surreys i.e. 10 filled ones & 10 empties.

'A' & 'B' Coys will carry their dixies, petrol tins, Lewis Guns by hand to new positions.

5. Completion of relief will be reported by code word "BATH".

6. On relief Companies will move to position indicated on map issued separately.

7. Arrival in new positions will be reported by code word "WASH".

8. Battn H.Q will be at D.21.b.6.3.

9. ACKNOWLEDGE

Copies to:
1. C.O
2. Adjt
3. O.C 'A' Coy
4. " 'B' "
5. " 'C' "
6. " 'D' "
7. R.S.M.
8. 10th Essex Regt.
9. 'A' Coy. 4th Bedfords.
10. Transport Officer
11. War Diary
12. File

2nd Lieutenant
4th Battn. R.W. Kent Regt

SECRET   Copy No.

          7th Bn R W Kent Regt
             Operation Order No. 18   APP. 93
Ref the Map D CORPS 1:5000   15.5.18.

1. **Intention** 7th R W Kent Regt is to carry out a Counter
attack Between front held by 55th Inf. Bde
E.7.d.9.c. to E.19.central

2. **Assembly Position** On enemy attack taking place
Battalion will move to assembly position in
E.11.d. and at once E.17.a.& c. when A & B Coys
are in position.
C Coy in assembly position in rear of B Coy
D " " " " in E.17.a. and South of
ACHIET ROAD.

3. **Disposition (Preliminary)**
   A & B Coys will carry out the assault
   A Coy on Left
   B   "   Right
   One platoon in 1st wave
   Two platoons in 2nd wave.
   C & D Coys in support.
   Scouts & follow up divisions will be
   detailed when attack develops.

4. **Tanks** 3 Tanks are at disposal to
assist the counter attack.

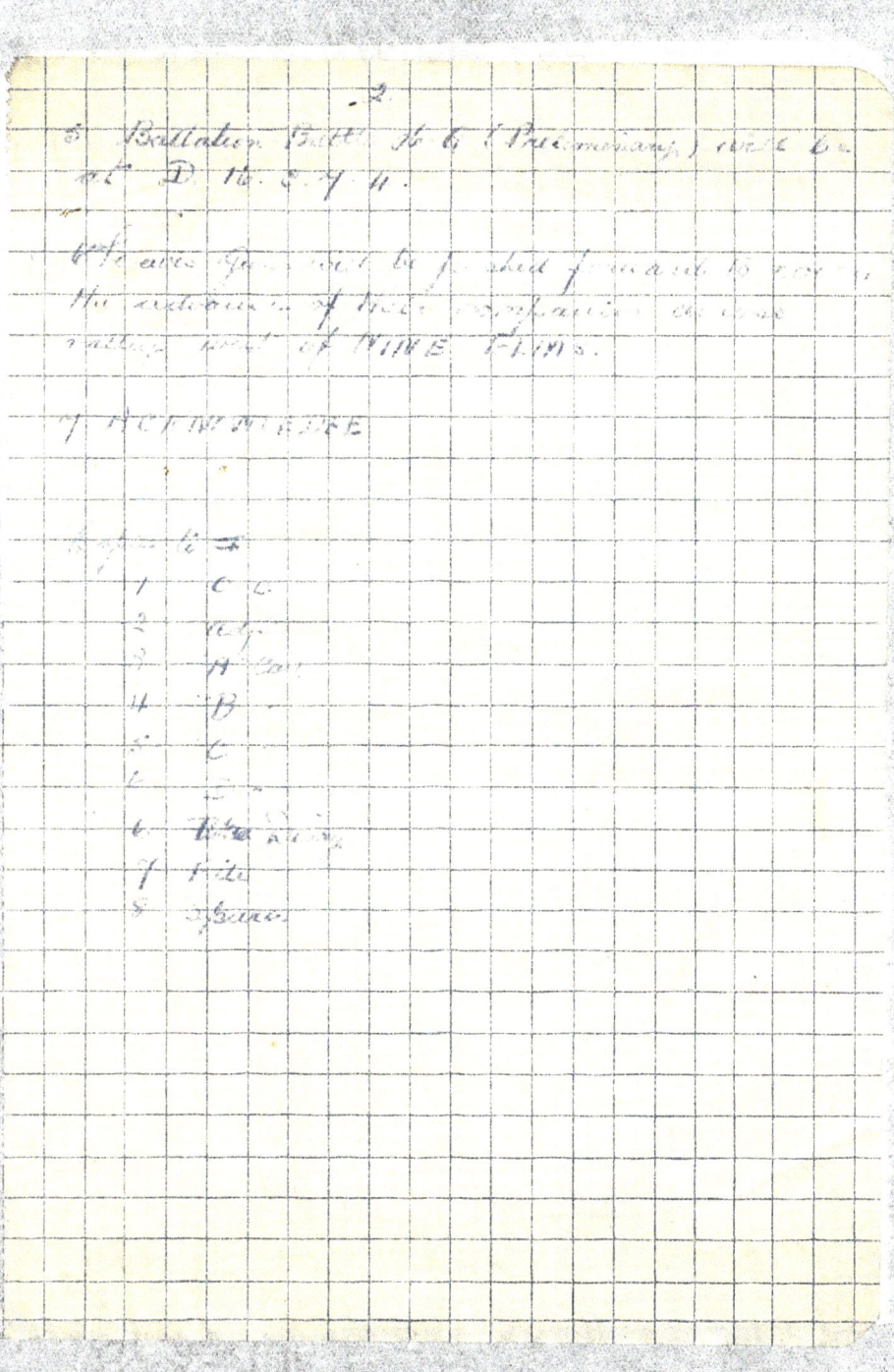

WAR DIARY
or
INTELLIGENCE SUMMARY.
(Erase heading not required.)

Army Form C. 2118.

7th R[oyal] W[est] Kent R[eg]t   June 18

Place	Date	Hour	Summary of Events and Information	Remarks and references to Appendices
Nr. CONTAY.	1-6-18.		Battalion relieved 2/4th. Battn. London Regt., in Left Battalion Sector of Left Brigade front. 2 Coys. in front line, 1 Coy. Counter attack, 1 Coy. Reserve.	APP. 102
In the LINE.	2-6-18.		Battalion holding Line. Improvement of Trenches. Practice anti-gas measures. Carrying party provided for R.E. Stores.	
	3-6-18.		Battalion holding Line. Reserve Company ("C" Coy.) relieved 2 Coys. 10th. Essex Regt., in front line. Repair and improvement of Trenches and Wire. Grass cutting in front of Posts. Improvement of Lewis Gun Posts.	APP. 103
	4-6-18.		Battalion holding Line. Repair and improvement of Trenches and Wire. Grass cutting in front of Posts. Improvement of Lewis Gun Posts. Battalion relieved by 11th. Battn. Royal Fusiliers and moved into Divisional Reserve at U.24.d.	APP. 104.
Near WARLOY.	5-6-18.		Battalion resting and cleaning up. Reconnaissance and allocation of duties whilst in Counter Attack positions. Warning Order to relieve in Right Brigade Sector on night of 8/9th. June.	APP. 105.
	6-6-18.		Training. Practice Skeleton Counter Attack.	APP. 106 a.b.
	7-6-18.		Training. Reconnaissance of Sector to be taken over. Battalion relieved 8th. Battn. East	APP. 107.
	8-6-18.		Training. Surrey Regiment as support Battalion in Right Brigade Sector of Divisional front.	APP. 108.
In the LINE.	9/11-6-18.		Improvement of Trenches. Work on dug-outs under R.E.	APP. 109.
	12-6-18.		-do- "B" Company moved to WARREGO Trench. No work with R.E. on account of 54th. and 53rd. Brigade operations.	
	13-6-18.		-do- Battalion relieved 10th. Battn. Essex Regt., in Left Battalion Sector, Right Brigade front.	APP. 110/11.
	14-6-18.		-do- "A" Company provided carrying party of 40 men for Stokes ammunition in connection with raid carried out by 8th. Royal Berks Regiment.	APP. 112.
	15-6-18.		-do- Inter Company reliefs. "A" Coy. relieved "C" Coy. in front Line	
	16-6-18.		-do- "D" " " "A" " in Support "C" " " "D" " Right reserve.	APP. 113.
	17/19-6-18.		Improvement of Trenches. Construction of fire steps.	
	20/21-6-18.		Battalion relieved by 8th. Battn. East Surrey Regt., and moved to Support positions in JAKES and COURT Trenches. "D" Company provided 1 Platoon to form first relay of working parties under 253 Tunnelling Company R.E.	APP. 114.
	22/23-6-18.		Cleaning up under Company arrangements. Working Parties under R.E. and improvement of JAKES Trench.	
	24-6-18.		Inspection of S.B.Rs. by Brigade Gas Officer. -do- -do-	

Army Form C. 2118.

WAR DIARY
or
INTELLIGENCE SUMMARY.
(Erase heading not required.)

Instructions regarding War Diaries and Intelligence Summaries are contained in F. S. Regs., Part II. and the Staff Manual respectively. Title pages will be prepared in manuscript.

Place	Date	Hour	Summary of Events and Information	Remarks and references to Appendices
In the LINE.	25-6-18.		Baths at WARLOY. Working Parties under R.E. and improvement of JAKES Trench.	APP. 115.
	26/27-6-18.		Working Parties under R.E. and improvement of JAKES Trench. Battalion relieved 8th. Battn. East Surrey Regiment in Left Battalion front, Right Brigade sector.	APP. 116.
	28/29-6-18.		Battalion holding Line. In connection with 53rd. Brigade's Chinese Attack at 9.35 p.m. "H.Q." and 2 Platoons "B" Company withdrawn from front Line; "D" Company carried out forward patrols during night.	
	30-6-18.		Battalion holding Line.	

OFFICERS' JOINED DURING MONTH.

2/Lieut. E.A.R. HEWITT.   Joined.   7-6-18.
2/Lieut. C.S. TURNER.   "   7-6-18.
2/Lieut. R.J. DICKINSON.   "   8-6-18.
Lieut. A.V.D. MORLEY, M.C., Rejoined. 23-6-18.

OFFICERS' CASUALTIES DURING MONTH.

Lieut. R.P. BUSH, M.C.,   Sick, to England from 24-5-18.
2/Lieut. L.P. SOLOMONS.   -do-   -do-   23-5-18.
Captain. C. STURLA.   -do-   -do-   24-4-18.
Lieut. A.V.D. MORLEY, M.C.,   Wounded. 14-6-18.
Lieut. N.G.S. SHEPPEY-GREENE.   Died of Wounds. 14-6-18.
2/Lieut. W.J. GODDARD, M.C.,   To England for employment with R.A.F. 17-6-18.
2/Lieut. C.W. HILL.   To England for duty with M.G. School, GRANTHAM 19-6-18.

Army Form C. 2118.

WAR DIARY
or
INTELLIGENCE SUMMARY.

(Erase heading not required.)

HONOURS AND AWARDS.

MILITARY CROSS.

2/Lieut. H.J.CHAPMAN. 8th. Norfolk Regiment attached 7th. Battn. Royal West Kent Regiment.

The G.O.C. the First French Army has been pleased to award the undermentioned decoration for gallantry during the attack on HANGARD on 12th. April. 1918.

CROIX DE GUERRE.

T/2nd. Lieut. R.P.WOODYEAR. M.C., 7th. Battalion Royal West Kent Regiment.

Lieut. Colonel.
Commanding 7th. Batalion Royal West Kent Regiment.

WAR DIARY
or
INTELLIGENCE SUMMARY.

(Erase heading not required.)

Army Form C. 2118.

7 RW Kent

Place	Date	Hour	Summary of Events and Information	Remarks and references to Appendices
In the LINE.	1-7-18.		"B" Coy. returned to Front Line after 53rd. Inf. Bde. Chinese Attacks. 1 O.R. Killed, 5 O.R. Wdd.	App. 117.
"	2-7-18.		Inter-Coy. reliefs.	App. 118.
"	3-7-18.		Hostile Artillery active. Gas on Front Line. 2 O.R. Wdd.	App. 118.A
"	4-7-18.		Test of direct S.O.S. fire by Lewis Guns in depth.	
"	5-7-18.		Gas Shells on Battalion Headquarters.	
"	6-7-18.		Front Line (except left platoon) cleared for Gas Shoot. Intermittent shelling W.26.a.b. Blue Cross and H.E. shells along MELBOURNE TRENCH. Battalion relieved by 8th. R. Berks. Regiment and becomes counter-attack Battalion. Relief complete 12.15 a.m. 7th. 1 O.R. Wdd.	App. 119.
"	8-7-18.		Mobilisation Order issued. One O.R. Wdd.	App. 119A.
"	9/10-7-18.		Situation Normal. 1 O.R. Wdd.	
"	11/12-7-18.		Battalion relieved by 18th. Battn. London Regt. Relief complete 2.0 a.m. 12th.	App. 120.
WARLOY.	12-7-18.		Battalion Embussed 4.0 a.m., arrived ST. PIERRE-A-GOUY 9.0 a.m.	
ST.PIERRE-A-GOUY.	13-7-18.		Battalion resting and cleaning up.	
"	14-7-18.		Battalion Training. Warning Order that Battalion is at present G.H.Q. Reserve and must be prepared to move at 9 hours notice.	App. 121.
"	15-7-18.		Battalion Training.	
"	16/22-7-18.		Battalion Training.	
"	23-7-18.		Battalion takes part in Brigade Route March, followed by demonstration of co-operation of Tanks and Infantry.	
"	24-7-18.		Battalion Training. Presentation of Medal Ribbons by Corps Commander.	
"	25-7-18.		Battalion Training. Warning Order received that 18th. Div. will relieve 58th. Div. in LINE on August 1st. and 2nd., 53rd. Inf. Bde. moving into reserve on the 2nd.	
"	26-7-18.		Battalion Training.	
"	27/29-7-18.		Battalion Training. Warning Order received 29th. for relief of 16th. R. Fusiliers EAST of LA HOUSSOYE.	
"	30-7-18.		Battalion Training. 44 Reinforcements, O.R.	
"	31-7-18.		Battalion Embussed at PICQUIGNY at 1.0 p.m. Debussed near PORT NOYELLES at 4.0 p.m. and Proceeded to Bivouacs SOUTH-EAST of LA HOUSSOYE, relieving 7 Bn. Queen's Regiment in reserve.	App. 122.

Army Form C. 2118.

WAR DIARY
or
INTELLIGENCE SUMMARY.
(Erase heading not required.)

Instructions regarding War Diaries and Intelligence Summaries are contained in F. S. Regs., Part II. and the Staff Manual respectively. Title pages will be prepared in manuscript.

Place	Date	Hour	Summary of Events and Information	Remarks and references to Appendices
	July 1918		**OFFICERS JOINED DURING THE MONTH.**	
			2/Lieut. L.J.TURNER. Joined. 9-7-18.	
			Lieut. A.BELL. Joined. 13-7-18.	
			2/Lieut. H.S.PEGLAR. Rejoined. 13-7-18.	
			2/Lieut. G.A.ATTEW. Joined. 18-7-18.	
			2/Lieut. G.A.BISHOP. Joined. 16-7-18.	
			2/Lieut. R.A.S.PHILLIPS. Joined. 22-7-18.	
			Capt. A.V.McDONALD.M.C., Rejoined 29-7-18.	
			Lieut. & Qr.M.A.H.GUY. Joined 29-7-18.	
			OFFICERS' CASUALTIES DURING THE MONTH.	
			Major A.F.NORTHCOTE. To England for Senior Officers' Course, ALDERSHOT, 2-7-18.	
			Major G.PLAYER. Marked "B.1" at Base, and Struck off strength. 2-7-18.	
			2/Lieut.R.LOVE. To England for duty with M.A.F., 15-7-18.	
			Lieut. & Qr.Mr. A.TAPP.M.C. To England for Tour of Duty. 22-7-18.	
			Lieut. W.RANKIN-JONES. To Base, Medically Unfit for Service at Front, 2-8-18	
			HONOURS & AWARDS.	
			MERITORIOUS SERVICE MEDAL. ------ No. 21992. Cpl. J.H.F.C.GUNNING. 14th Bn.Gloster Regt., attd., 7th R.W.Kent Regt.	
			------000------	
			[signature] Major.	
			Commanding 7th Battalion Royal West Kent Regt.	

Army Form C. 2118.

WAR DIARY
or
INTELLIGENCE SUMMARY.
(Erase heading not required.)

7th Battn. ROYAL WEST KENT REGT.

Instructions regarding War Diaries and Intelligence Summaries are contained in F.S. Regs., Part II. and the Staff Manual respectively. Title pages will be prepared in manuscript.

Place	Date	Hour	Summary of Events and Information	Remarks and references to Appendices
Near LA HOUSSOYE.	1/6-8-18.		Battalion role, - (a) Counter-attack on any part of Divisional Front, (b) Permanent Garrison of FRANVILLERS SYSTEM. TRAINING.	
	6-8-18.		Battalion moved at 8.45 p.m. to occupy ROMA LINE from SOMME to BRAY -- CORBIE Road (Inclusive).	App.123.
	7-8-18.		Battalion moved to assembly position for attack at Dusk.	App.124.
	8-8-18.		Barrage opened 4.20 a.m. Dense Fog. Battalion advanced in artillery formation from BURKE TRENCH. Enemy Machine Guns were encountered causing loss of time and direction. Final objective not reached. Casualties.Officers - Killed 2, Wounded 6. O.Rs. - Killed 198.	App.125.
	9-8-18.		Battalion holding front line.	
	10-8-18.		Battalion relieved and moved to billets in BAIZIEUX.	
	11-8-18.		Battalion relieved 15th. Battn. LONDON Regiment in Support on centre subsector of III Corps front on night of 11/12th. August, 1918.	App.126.
	12/13-8-18.		Battalion in Support.	
Nr. HENENCOURT.	14-8-18.		Battalion in Reserve. Baths in HENENCOURT.	App.127.
	15-8-18.		Battalion relieved 8th. Battn. Royal Berks Regt., in Left Sector of Brigade Sector.	App.127a.
	16-8-18.		Inter-Company reliefs.	App.128.
	17/18-8-18.		Battalion relieved by 8th. Battn. East Surrey Regt., and moved to shelters in HALLULE VALLEY.	
Nr. WARLOY.	19/21-8-18.		Battalion resting and re-fitting.	App.129.
	22-8-18.		Battalion moved at 8.0 a.m. to V.27.c. and D.3.b.	App.129a &
	23-8-18.		Battalion attacked with tanks and barrage. Barrage opened 4.45 a.m. Objectives gained and consolidated. Casualties -- included in following day's total.	130.
	24-8-18.		Battalion less two Coys. attacked. Barrage opened 1.0 a.m. Objectives gained and consolidated. Casualties.-- Officers 8, O.Rs. 142.	App.130a. & 131
	25-8-18.		Battalion relieved by 7th. Battn. The BUFFS and withdrawn to WEST of ALBERT.	App.132.
	26-8-18.		Battalion moved forward to BECOURT and from thence to SOUTH of MAMETZ WOOD.	App.132a.
	27-8-18.		"D" Coy. acting with 10th. Battn. ESSEX Regt. took part in attack at 8.0 p.m. on EASTERN Edge of TRONES WOOD from light railway to SOUTH Extremity. Casualties - Officers 1, O.Rs. 89.	
	28-8-18.		Battalion relieved by 6th. Battn. NORThampton Regt.	App.133.
	29-8-18.		Battalion moved to garrison positions in T.27.a. & c. and T.26.	App.134.
	30-8-18.		Battalion moved to line, WEDGE WOOD - GINCHY ROAD - EAST of Guillemont.	App.135.
	31-8-18.		Battalion holding permanent Garrison Line in T.27.a.7.7. to T.21.c.4.7.	

Army Form C. 2118.

WAR DIARY
or
INTELLIGENCE SUMMARY.
(Erase heading not required.)

Instructions regarding War Diaries and Intelligence Summaries are contained in F. S. Regs., Part II. and the Staff Manual respectively. Title pages will be prepared in manuscript.

Place	Date	Hour	Summary of Events and Information	Remarks and references to Appendices
	AUGUST, 1918.		**OFFICERS' JOINED DURING THE MONTH.**	
			Captain. T.L.TANNER. Joined 3-8-18.	
			Lieut. J.C.COBB. " 3-8-18.	
			2/Lieut. E.C.MONTAGUE. " 5-8-18.	
			2/Lieut. A.HODGKINSON. " 12-8-18.	
			2/Lieut. A.W.JONES. " 12-8-18.	
			2/Lieut. R.B.L.HILL. " 12-8-18.	
			2/Lieut. C.J.WOOLLEY. " 12-8-18.	
			2/Lieut. A.W.C.WINGFIELD. " 12-8-18.	
			2/Lieut. J.H.FELL. " 14-8-18.	
			2/Lieut. R.K.WATTS. " 14-8-18.	
			2/Lieut. R.H.PIGOU. " 14-8-18.	
			2/Lieut. W.S.CLARIDGE. " 21-8-18.	
			2/Lieut. P.D.BERTRAM. Rejoined from T.M.B. 14-8-18.	
			Captain. F.H.SOLOMON. Joined 23-8-18.	
			Major. S.W.WARR. Joined 26-8-18.	
			Captain. F.T.KIRK. " 27-8-18.	
			2/Lieut. B.M.OLIVER. " 27-8-18.	
			2/Lieut. M.J.CLAPHAM. " 27-8-18.	
			2/Lieut. H.A.DEBENHAM. " 27-8-18.	
			2/Lieut. J.S.LARKEN. " 27-8-18.	
			2/Lieut. A.F.NEILL. " 27-8-18.	
			2/Lieut. P.J.PETER. " 27-8-18.	
			2/Lieut. B.HOWLETT. " 28-8-18.	
			2/Lieut. F.AXTELL. M.M. " 30-8-18.	
			Lieut. L.JONES. " 31-8-18.	
			Lieut. G.C.S.BASKETT. " 31-8-18.	
			OFFICERS' CASUALTIES DURING THE MONTH.	
			Lieut. F.LINDSEY-JONES. To BASE, marked B.II, and struck off strength. Proceeded to BASE 2-8-18.	
			2/Lieut. R.A.S.PHILLIPS. To 7th. Battn. The BUFFS Regt., 4-8-18.	
			2/Lieut. H.J.CHAPMAN. M.C. Killed in Action 8-8-18.	
			Lieut. A. HACKFORTH-JONES. " " 8-8-18.	
			Lieut. A.V.D.MORLEY. M.C. Wounded " 8-8-18.	
			Lieut. B.BERGL. " " 8-8-18.	
			Lieut. A.BELL. " " 8-8-18.	
			2/Lieut. W.F.CHAPMAN. " " 8-8-18.	
			2/Lieut. C.R.ADDISON. " " 8-8-18.	
			Lieut. J.C.COBB. Killed " 23-8-18.	
			2/Lieut. R.K.WATTS. " " 23-8-18.	
			2/Lieut. W.H.DESPREZ " " 24-8-18.	
			2/Lieut. E.C.MONTAGUE. Wounded " 23-8-18.	
			2/Lieut. A.HODGKINSON. " " 23-8-18.	

Army Form C. 2118.

WAR DIARY
or
INTELLIGENCE SUMMARY.

(*Erase heading not required.*)

OFFICERS' CASUALTIES DURING THE MONTH. (CONTINUED).

2/Lieut. R.H.PIGOU.   Wounded (At duty). 23-8-18.
2/Lieut. G.H.FELL.   Wounded in Action   23-8-18.
2/Lieut. W.S.CLARIDGE.   "   "   23-8-18.
2/Lieut. G.HUMPAGE.   "   "   27-8-18.

P. Brown
Major,
Commanding 7th. Battalion Royal West Kent Regiment.

APP 123
APP 123

SECRET.   Copy No. 2

7th. Battalion Royal West Kent Regiment.

OPERATION ORDER NO. 23.

6th. August. 1918.

1. The Battalion will move to-night at 8.45 p.m. to be permanent garrison of the ROMA LINE from the SOMME to BRAY -- CORBIE Road (inclusive).

2. DISPOSITIONS.
"D" Company from BRAY -- CORBIE Road (inclusive) to J.22.b.9.0.
"C" Company from J.22.b.9.0 to J.22.d.7.0.
"A" Company from J.22.d.7.0. to J.28.d.2.8.
The positions will be held with 3 Platoons in front Line and one in elements behind.
"B" Company will be in reserve in trench elements in J.21.b. and J.22.a.
Battalion Headquarters and Aid Post will be in banks in J.21.c.
"D" Company will get into touch with the 7th. Battn. Queen's Regt., on their left, and report to Headquarters when this has been done.
Company Commanders will as soon as possible, check all Trench Stores in their Line.

3. ROUTE. The Battalion will march via BONNAY, thence by BONNAY -- MERICOURT Road to J.13.b.7.7. J.14.c.5.0. -- J.15.central -- J.22.central, except "B" Company who will turn off at J.22.a.
ORDER OF MARCH. :-   Time of start.
           "A" Company............................8.45 p.m.
           "D" Company............................8.55 p.m.
           "C" Company............................9. 5 p.m.
           "B" Company............................9.15 p.m.
           "H.Q." Company.
The BRAY -- CORBIE Road will be avoided as far as possible.

4. DRESS. :- As already ordered.

5. TRANSPORT.   1 Lewis Gun Limber per Company and 1 Limber for "H.Q." will at Company Headquarters at 8.0 p.m. to-night.

6. Police are be stationed at CROSS ROADS J.13.b. and J.15.central.

7. Arrival in position will be reported to Battalion Headquarters by Runner which will be the means of communication until telephones are established.

8. Transport Lines will remain in present location.

Issued at...7.30...p.m.

(Signed:-) L.F.S. SPALDING,
Captain and Adjutant,
7th. Battalion Royal West Kent Regiment.

SECRET.   Copy No...1...

7th. Battalion Royal West Kent Regiment.

OPERATION ORDER NO.21.

Ref. Map
Sheet 62.D., N.E.   5th. August. 1918.

1. The 18th. Division will attack in conjunction with troops on the right and will capture the line as shown on map already issued. Date and hour of attack will be notified later.

2. The attack will be made in two phases.
    1st. Phase.
    54th. and 55th. Infantry Brigades will capture and consolidate ground up to the first objective — the BLUE LINE.
    2nd. Phase.
    53rd. Infantry Brigade will advance through the 54th. and 55th. Infantry Brigades and will capture the final objective — the RED LINE.

3. Objectives and boundaries are shown on map already issued.

4. The attack by the 53rd. Infantry Brigade will be carried out in two bounds as shown on map "D".
    1st. Bound.
    10th. Essex Regt. on the right, and 7th. R.W. Kent Regt., on the left, will capture the intermediate objective — the BLACK LINE.
    2nd. Bound.
    8th. R. Berks Regt. on the right and 10th. Essex Regt. on the left, will capture the final objective — the RED LINE.

5. The attack will be carried out with Tanks under barrage. There will be no preliminary bombardment.

6. TANKS. Two Coys., 10th. Battalion Tanks will work with the Brigade. For detail see appendix "B".

7. ARTILLERY. Barrage will move at rate of 100 yards in 4 minutes throughout.

8. MACHINE GUNS. "A" Company (16 guns), 18th. Battalion Machine Gun Corps, is attached to 53rd. Inf. Bde. for the operation.
These will take up positions as shown on map "D".
Two guns will move forward immediately behind "A" Company and two guns immediately behind "C" Company.

9. TRENCH MORTARS. Two T.M's and 100 rounds per gun are allotted to the Battalion. Dispositions of these will be notified later.

10. R,E. and PIONEERS. 1 Coy. R.E. and 1 Coy. Pioneers are allotted to the Brigade for the consolidation of the GREEN LINE.

11. ASSEMBLY. The initial positions of assembly are :-
    "C" Coy. in 300 yards of BURKE TRENCH immediately NORTH of CORBIE — BRAY Road in K.13.c.
    "A" Coy. in 300 yards of BURKE TRENCH immediately SOUTH of CORBIE — BRAY Road in K.19.a.
    "D" Coy. in 300 yards of COBAR TRENCH immediately NORTH of CORBIE — BRAY Road in K.13.c.
    "B" Coy. in elements of Trenches in J.18.d. NORTH of CORBIE — BRAY Road.

12. DISPOSITIONS. From assembly positions to time of arrival of final objective are shown on map "D".

2.

13: **THE ATTACK.**
The Battalion will move from its assembly positions at ZERO plus 30, and will form up on BLUE LINE(map "D"), which the 54th. Brigade will be holding. Movement will be by Coys. in Artillery Formation of Platoons at 150 yards interval and 100 yards distance. Inner Platoons will be at 100 yards from road. Movement will be at the rate of 100 yards in 3 minutes which will bring the Battalion to BLUE LINE at ZERO plus 90. (Inner Platoons will guide). The barrage will then be 250 yards in front of BLUE LINE. at ZERO plus 115 the barrage will intensify and the Battalion will move forward in worms of sections at 50 yards interval and 50 yards distance to as close as possible to the barrage which will lift at ZERO plus 130, when the troops will pass straight through to their final objective.

Each Company and Platoon Commander will carry a Yellow Flag, and at ZERO plus 115, each will jump up and show his Flag as a signal for advance to begin.

Every Platoon will be given a definite objective to which it will push on. On no account will a general halt be made should a portion of the line be checked.

CONSOLIDATION.
On arrival at the final objective, Outposts previously detailed will move out at once to cover the consolidation. The Outpost Line will be a line of resistance as as such, all posts will be dug in.

The RED LINE will be consolidated in depth by a series of Platoon Strong Points well dug in and wired, and sited for mutual support.

As soon as the consolidation is completed, the line will be thinned out to the minimum number of men consistent with security. The remaining troops will be distributed in depth, and will be held available to renforce or counter-attack under orders of Battalion Commander.

The retention of the high ground round the BRICKYARD is of special importance. "B" Company will be held in reserve for counter-attack on this point.

Roads leading into the position must be covered by Lewis Gun fire.

Coy. Commanders and all ranks are reminded of the great importance of constant communication with Battalion Headquarters, as to positions reached, and subsequent situations.

14. **ENEMY COUNTER-ATTACKS.**
All information as to possible counter-attacks will be issued personally to Company Commanders.

15. **ENEMY RUSES.**
All troops will be specially warned against the various ruses which may be employed by the enemy :-
    Misuse of the White Flag.
    Shamming Death,
    Use of English Words of Command, such as "RETIRE".
    Machine Guns on Stretchers.
the word "RETIRE" will not be used. Any Officer or man giving this command will be shot at once.

16. **COMMUNICATIONS.** See appendix "E".

17. **DRESS.** Fighting Order. 120 rounds S.A.A. (Signallers and Runners, 50 rounds each). IN PACK. :- Iron Ration; W.P. Sheet; Knife, fork, spoon; pair Socks; Emergency Oil Can; 4" by 2"; Mess-tin.
IN HAVERSACK.:- Day's Ration; Waterbottle, filled.
Rifle Bombers will carry 4 No.36 grenades.
"A" and "C" Coys. will carry 100 No.23 grenades each. } In men's
"B" and "D" " " " 50 No.23 " " } Haversacks.
Lewis Gun Sections will carry Entrenching Tool,
Rifle Sections will carry Picks and Shovels in proportion of 40% Picks, 60% Shovels.
Company and Platoon Headquarters will carry a Very Light Pistol each and 6 Lights each.

3.

17. (Continued).
Tin Discs for signalling to Aeroplanes will be distributed to Coys. and carried by each section equally.

18. ADMINISTRATIVE INSTRUCTIONS.   Will be issued separately under Appendix "F".

19. SYNCHRONIZATION OF WATCHES.   Instructions will be issued later.

20. ACKNOWLEDGE.

Issued at *Midnight*.

(Signed:-) L.F.S. SPALDING,
Captain and Adjutant,
7th. Battalion Royal West Kent Regiment.

----------oOo----------

Appendix "B".

TANKS.

5 sections i.e., 20 Tanks, will be operating with the first attack.

After the capture of the first objective they will re-form on the line of the track immediately WEST of the BLUE LINE and will move forward at ZERO plus 130 with the 53rd. Infantry Brigade.

Tanks will work in sections, each Section with 3 Tanks in the front line and one behind.

The most advanced Infantry Sections will move between, or immediately in rear of the leading line of Tanks. They will not actually follow individual Tanks, as the Tanks will take a zigzag course in order to ensure as far as possible the whole ground being covered.

Infantry must not be led away from their objectives by Tanks.

One selected Infantry N.C.O. will be in each Tank.   His duty will be to watch the Infantry and to keep the Tank Commander informed as to their progress.

Four N.C.O's from each Battalion for this purpose will report to Headquarters, 10th. Battalion Tanks, HEILLY, on the afternoon of "Y" day.

Each fighting Tank will carry two Pigeons and 5 boxes of S.A.A. on the back of the Tank.

Unit Commanders will arrange to take all this S.A.A. from the Tanks before they return to their rendezvous.

After the capture of the final objective and when the covering troops in front are established in position, one Company of Tanks will be withdrawn to the valley in K.21. for the purpose of counter-attack. Battalions will have a direct call on these Tanks for assistance if required.

The following signals will be used :-
From Tanks to Infantry.
(I)   A Green and White Flag to indicate "COME ON".
(II) A Red and Yellow Flag to indicate "I AM BROKEN DOWN, GO ON".
(III) A Tricolour Flag to indicate "TANK IS RETURNING OUT OF ACTION", and to prevent its being mistaken for an enemy Tank.

4.

Infantry to Tanks.

Steel Helmets waved on the ends of Bayonets and pointing in the required direction, or smoke bombs, will indicate to Tanks that "ASSISTANCE IS REQUIRED".

---oOo---

Two Tanks have been detailed to deal solely with the BRICKYARD. One Tank to work on "D" Coys. front, one Tank to work on "A" Coys. front and one TANK will go direct to K.17.central.

One carrying Tank has been detailed to bring up S.A.A., Food, Water, etc., which it will distribute direct to Coys. 2/Lt.W.A.SHEARING will be in charge of the stores on this Tank and will superintend distribution.

Tanks carry a semaphore Arm. All signallers should be on the look-out for signals from it.

---oOo---

Appendix. "E"

COMMUNICATIONS.

Battle H.Q.

18th. Battalion M.G.C.	J.17.d.2.4.
53rd. Infantry Brigade.	J.24.b.8.8., moving when situation permits to vicinity of K.21.c.0.0.
8th. R. Berks Regt.	Vicinity of K.23.c.6.2.
10th. Essex. Regt.	
7th. Bn. R.W. Kent Regt.	At K.22.central.

Battalion Headquarters will be marked by Signal Flags.

1. **TELEPHONE.**
    During and after the attack of 53rd. Brigade, cable will be run and maintained to the Battalion Headquarters.
    "A", "C" and "B" Coys. will have Lucas Lamps, Flags and Folding Shutters for inter-communication between Coys. and to Battalion Headquarters where ground permits. "B" Company will probably act as relay station to Battalion Headquarters.

2. **RUNNERS.** Must study all enemy tracks etc., from map.

---oOo---

CONTACT AEROPLANES.

Will call for signals from the Infantry by sounding the Claxon Horn. The most advanced Infantry only will respond to his call by showing the tin disc with which the men will be supplied, or by laying Rifles in parallel groups of 3 on the parapet of any trench.

Discs should be laid flat on the ground, bright side upwards, when Aeroplane calls by letter "A's". Otherwise they should be laid painted side up.

COUNTER-ATTACK AEROPLANES.

Will indicate the direction of an enemy assembly or counter-attack by sounding the Claxon Horn and by firing a White Parachute Flare in the direction of the enemy advance.

---oOo---

Map 'C'

Black line
Line means Objective
Barrage lifts 14 minutes on front of divisions on 8 minutes on 1st objective in 4 minutes

Red Objective

220-228
212-220
204-212
196-204
188-196
180-188
172-180

172

154-158
150-154
146-150
142-146
138-142
134-138
130-134
130

Green Objective

Div Bndy
Div Bndy

Reg. Sheet 62 N.E. 1/20,000

APPENDIX "D".

ATTACK WITH ARTILLERY BARRAGE AND TANKS.

This is a diagram only. Once the column is in motion, the action of the Infantry must conform to ground, fire opposition and fire effect, and must not be dependent upon the tanks.

Artillery Barrage (shrapnel).

About 30x.

2 sections of Tanks manoeuvring at 7 miles per hour, and advancing at the rate of the barrage, starting with an interval of from 75x to 100x between Tanks and forming a screen to the Infantry.

25x to 50x normally, but sections of Infantry to seize any opportunity and not to hesitate to move forward between the Tanks.

Leading platoons in section columns with scouts out. Platoons to advance straight to their front and not to follow individual Tanks but seize opportunities afforded by Tanks which happen to be in front of them at any particular time. Platoons have got to bayonet the frightened Boche hiding from the tank or shoot the frightened Boche running away from it; the tanks cannot be relied on to do this.

[Diagram showing platoons in ovals with L.G. markings: 1 platoon, L.G. / 1 platoon, L.G. / L.G., 1 platoon / 1 platoon, L.G. / L.G., 1 platoon]

50x.

Reserve Tank to replace casualties.

Reserve Tank to replace casualties.

Platoons formed up in depth as required for Bn. scheme of attack.

Platoons will be in section or platoon columns as dictated by hostile artillery and M.G. fire.

The following signals will be used from Tanks to Infantry.
(i) A green and white flag to indicate "Come on".
(ii) A red and yellow flag to indicate "I am broken down, go on".
(iii) A tricolour flag to indicate that the Tank is returning out of action and prevent its being mistaken for an enemy tank.

NOT TO BE TAKEN BEYOND FRONT LINE TRENCHES.

NARRATIVE OF ATTACK ON 8/8/18

REF. MAP 62? N.E. N5 APP. 125

On 5th August 1918 the 7th BATT'N ROYAL WEST KENT REGT. was ordered to take part in an attack on the morning of the 8th in conjunction with the other Battalions of the Brigade. The 10th ESSEX REGT. on the RIGHT and the 55 BRIGADE forming a FLANK on the LEFT as the ATTACK proceeded.

The assembly positions allotted were as follows:- A. COY. in BUNBURY TRENCH from J.18.C.4.3. to J.18.C.8.8. C. COY. from ROSS COMMUNICATION TRENCH in J.18.a. D COY in MANLY COMMUNICATION TRENCH J.17.b+d. B COY in MANLY SUPPORT in J.17.d. BATT'N H.QRs in STRONG POINT at J.17.c.

The objective of the BATTALION was to form a FLANK facing NORTH from K.15.d.0.5 to K.16.d.9.5. joining up with the 7th QUEENS REGT. on the LEFT and the 10th ESSEX REGT on the RIGHT. Companies were allotted the following objectives D. Coy. from K.15.d.0.5 to K.16.c.1.6. C. COY. from K.16.c.1.6. to K.16.d.1.7. A COY. K.16.d.1.7 to K.16.d.9.5. B COY in SUPPORT from K.16.c.5.0 to K.16.d.4.0.

2.

At 4.20AM on the 8th August 1918 the BARRAGE opened and the BATTALION advanced in ARTILLERY FORMATION by platoons. Almost immediately a dense fog came down and it was impossible to see more than 20 yards ahead. The advance until the leading Companies reached BURKE STREET was carried out in good order. A. Coy having moved to the SOUTH SIDE of the BRAY-CORBIE ROAD in accordance with orders. From here onwards parties of the enemy and machine guns were encountered in every direction which caused considerable amount of fighting and great loss of time and loss of direction.

Eventually at about 7 AM about 200 men comprising largely this BATTALION and parties of ESSEX and BERKS were formed up astride the BRAY-CORBIE ROAD from about K.14.c.5.5. to K.20.a.5.5. with a FLANK thrown back along COMMUNICATION TRENCH to about K.13.d.3.8.

Touch could not be obtained anywhere with the 55 BRIGADE and very little could be ascertained of the Troops

3

in Front. As it appeared that our NORTHERN FLANK was entirely exposed the situation was reported by an officer to the BRIGADE, and the BATTN was then ordered to form a NORTHERN FLANK on the BLUE LINE and to get astride the BRAY-CORBIE ROAD. Considerable number of the enemy were found in COMMUNICATION TRENCH running from K.14.c.46 to K.14.d.94 but this line was eventually made good, and the line from K.14.d.94 to the BRAY-CORBIE ROAD at K.21.a.18 was taken up, where touch was obtained with the 10th BATTN ESSEX REGT.

In the meantime a portion of B.COY. by hugging the road reached the BLUE LINE in time, in accordance with orders and advanced with the BARRAGE with the assistance of two tanks.

The BRICKYARD was attacked and a line established linking up with the 10th BN. ESSEX REGT. on the RIGHT at K.15.d.95. At about 10 oclock the enemy attacked on both FLANKS which were exposed and the C.O. of the 10th ESSEX REGT. decided to

4.

withdraw to the BLUE LINE SOUTH of the BRAY CORBIE ROAD this was carried out.

Owing to the dense fog the tanks and the advanced troops were unable to clear the ground up to the BLUE LINE and the BATTN in consequence had to fight its way through, what made it impossible to form up on that LINE more or less intact as was anticipated.

During the afternoon at 3.45p.m. the enemy attempted a COUNTER ATTACK from about K11 Central to K10d.0.8. but failed to reach our FRONT LINE.

This line was firmly established and held until the 9th August 1918 when other troops continued the advance.

SECRET.   10-8-18

Operation Order No. 30   APP.125A

1. Battalion will move to billets in BAIZIEUX to-night, 10th August commencing 7-30.
Route:- BRAY-CORBIE ROAD to CROSS ROADS J.16.d.2.0 - MERICOURT - RIBEMONT thence direct.

2. Order of march:- 'C' Coy. H.Qrs. D. B & A Coys. 'C' Coy. will move direct to Bde. H.Q. leaving the main BRAY-CORBIE ROAD at least 200 yards on the NORTH. 'D. B & A' Coys. will move via Bn. H.Q. where guides will meet them. Platoons will move at least 100 yds. Distance. Lewis Guns & Magazines will be loaded on Limbers at J.24.b.8.8. Guides for Billets will be at CROSS ROADS, SOUTH-EAST Corner of BAIZIEUX.

(Signd.) W.A. SHEARING 2/Lt
A/ADJT.
VOVU

CROSS
J.20 Cent R.19 Cent

SECRET   APP. 126   COPY NO. 11
7th Battn Royal West Kent Regt

OPERATION ORDER No. 31

APP. 126

11 Aug 1918

1. The 7th Battn R W Kent Regt will relieve 15th Bn LONDON Regt in Support in the centre Sub Sector in the Left Sector of the III Corps front on the night of 11/12 Aug. 1918.
   The 129th AMERICAN Battn is on the RIGHT and the 52nd Inf Bde on the LEFT.

2. GUIDES from the Battn relieved will meet the Battn at the QUARRY D.4.c.2.3 at 9.58 pm

3. An Advance Party of 2/Lt SHEARING and 1 Senior NCO per Coy will report at present Battn HQ at 2.0 pm to meet guides at D.4.c.2.3 at 3.0 pm

4. All Defence Schemes, maps, aeroplane maps, A P Ammunition, S O S, Grenades, message rockets &c will be taken over & copies of receipts given will reach the O.R. by 12.0 noon 12th inst
   Particular attention will be paid

2.

to the taking over of patrol schemes
& work in hand

5. Head of Battn will pass BAZIEUX
Church at 8.55 pm
 Order of March A Coy – B Coy – C Coy –
  D Coy – HQ Coy.
 50 yds interval between platoons.
 16 L.G. magazines per gun will be
 carried on ~~the man~~
 2 S.O.S. Rockets will be taken in
 10 L.G. magazines per gun will be dumped
 at Battn HQ by 8.0 pm

6. TRANSPORT. 2 Lewis Gun limbers and
two ~~no limbers~~ for ~~mess stores~~ battle stores, signal stores
 & HQ mess box will report at Battn
 HQ at 8.0 pm.
  Coy mess box etc will travel on Lewis
 Gun limber

7. One Officer, one runner & 1 NCO
 per platoon will reconnoitre tracks from
 BAZIEUX to D.4.c.2.3. by daylight

8. 1 Pint of Hot Tea & 1 Pint of cold tea
 & 1 Pint of Water per man, will be
 sent up by Transport tonight
  Next days rations will be taken
 in on the man.

3

9. Completion of relief will be notified to Battn HQ by the message "Order No. 31 complied with", and time.

10. Officers' Valises etc will be dumped at A M Stores at 6.0 pm tonight

11. ACKNOWLEDGE

Issued at 3.0 pm   (Sd) L.F.S Spalding Capt
                              Adjutant
                         2nd Bn R W Kent Regt

Copy No 1. CO.
       2. Adjutant
       3. OC 'A' Coy
       4. OC 'B' Coy
       5. OC 'C' Coy
       6. OC 'D' Coy
       7. OC HQ Coy
       8. T.O
       9. QM
       10. RSM
       11. File
       12. War Diary

APP SECRET.   File APP 127 Copy No. 11
APP
127
             7th Battn Royal West Kent Regt.
             OPERATION ORDER No 32   14/8/18

1. The 7th Battn R.W. KENT REGT will
relieve the 8th R. BERKS REGT in
the LEFT SECTOR of the BRIGADE
SECTOR on the NIGHT 14th/15th Aug 1918

2. DISPOSITIONS
       B Coy R.W.K.R will relieve A Coy 8th R.BERKS
       C   "   "   "   "   "   B " 8th   "
       D   "   "   "   "   "   D " 8th   "
       A   "   "   "   "   "   C " 8th   "

3. GUIDES Four guides per Coy and two for Bn
H.QRS will be at the D.S. Y.23.C.3.6 at 10.0 PM

4. All maps, Aeroplane Photos, defence Schemes
Trench Stores etc. will be taken over & copies
of receipts will be sent to O.R by 9. am
15/8/18. Defence Arrangements as handed
over will be adhered to until further orders
Especial Attention will be paid to patrol Schemes
of advanced Coy. and scheme of work in
hand. S.O.S. Rockets will be taken into
the line and will not be handed over
as Trench Stores

5. Advanced parties of Lieut Phipps and Sgt
RAFFERTY for B.H.Q. and one Officer and

2

one NCO per Coy and proceed to new
position at 8.0 pm and take over

6. Cooking Arrangements. Rations for advanced
Coy. will be cooked at Transport Lines.
Other Coys & H.Q. will cook their rations
in the Trenches. The park of the Company
relieving advanced Coy will take over
the cooking of the relieved Company.
B Coy will be in advanced position
first.

7. TRANSPORT. 1 hand cart per Coy for Lewis Gun
+ Cooking utensils, 2 limbers for H.Q.
for stores etc, will be at present
Batt. position at 9.0 pm tonight.
Rations will be dumped as follows
H.Q at V30.6.3.4. for Companies
at Coy H.Q. except advanced Company
who will make their own arrangements

8. COMPLETION OF RELIEF will be notified
by phone by the message "ORDER Nº 32
Complied with. Name of Coy to be added

9. Bn H.Q. at V30.6.3.4
    R.A.P. at V30.6.1.4

Issued at 3.15 am   SD L SPALDING Capt
                        Adjutant
                     7th Bn R.W.Kent R.

SECRET.   APP 127A
OPERATION ORDER N°33

1. C.Coy will relieve B.Coy in the FRONT LINE tonight, all arrangements to be made between the Coys concerned as to GUIDES ETC.,

2. RATIONS for B.Coy will be received by C.Coy and vice versa. Officers Rations and mail will be transferred at BATTN. H.QRS. below the limbers proceed forward.

3. COMPLETION OF RELIEF will be notified to BATTALION H.QRS. by the code word "GEE WHIZ" and time.

4. B.Coy will continue the work of putting crops as soon as they are in position.

5. The AMERICAN platoons will not move but will be relieved later on, by another Company of AMERICANS. Arrangements will be made between the two American Company Commanders.

"Each Company will send 1 British guide along with one American guide to report to Battalion H.QRs 7 pm to-night"

Issued at within
Copies to
 H.M
 B
 C
 D
 [illegible]
 File

SECRET   W. DIARY   APP/2 COPY NO 1/

APP/13

7 BATT.N ROYAL WEST KENT REGT
OPERATION ORDER No 34

August 17th 18

1. The Tactical situation permitting the 7th Batt.n Royal West Kent Regiment will be relieved by the 8th Batt.n East Surrey Regiment in the LEFT BATT.N FRONT of the CENTRE BRIGADE SECTOR on the Night 17th/18th August 1918. as follows:—

   "C" Coy 7th R.W.Kent Regt relieved by "D" Coy 8th E.Surrey
   "B"   "   "   "   "   "   "   "A"   " 8th E.SURREY
   "D"   "   "   "   "   "   "   "B"   " 8th E.SURREY
   "A"   "   "   "   "   "   "   "C"   " 8th E.SURREY

2. All Defence Schemes, Trench Stores, message Rockets, and details of work and and projected, including the cutting of CROPS will be handed over and receipts forwarded to Batt.n H.Q. by 12 NOON 18th August 1918. S.O.S Rockets will NOT be handed over but will be carried out.

3. Party of A.Coy. now working on Tunnelled dug-out will be relieved at 8 A.M. the 18th August by a party from 8th BATT.N E SURREY REGIMENT

2

4. AMERICAN Platoons attached to Companies will be handed over in Situ together with any correspondence etc. concerning their relief and attachment.

5. GUIDES to the proportion of two for BATTN H.QRS, one per Company HQRs. and one per British platoon will report at Battn HQ. to 2/Lieut A.W.G. WINGFIELD 8 PM 17th August 1918.

6. On RELIEF Companies will proceed to shelters in River Valley V.19d qua BATTN. HQRS and TRACK running through V.24C 23cd to a point on the TRACK in V.20d, where guides will be met to lead Companies to Shelters

7. Transport Arrangements
2 Limbers will be at BATTN HQRS at 10.30pm
1 Limber will report to each Coy HQrs at 10.30pm. Except "C" Coy whose Limber will be on the road at E.2a.4.8 at 10.30pm and will wait till the Company comes out.

8. All empty petrol tins and Haypacks will be taken out

9. Completion of Relief will be reported to Battalion HQRS by the code phrase "CIGARETTES WANTED BADLY" and time

Issued at 5.0 P.M.
Copies to
No 1 C.O.
   2 Adjt
   3 O/c A Coy
   4   " B "
   5   " C "
   6   " D "
   7   R.S.M.
   8 O/c Bombers Sigs & Regt
   9   T.O
  10   Q.M
  11   War Diary
  12   File

(SIGNED)
C.C. THOMSON Lieut
For Adjutant
4 Batt. R.W.K. Regt.

APP 129 APP 129

SECRET.   Copy No. 2.

7th. Battalion Royal West Kent Regiment.

WARNING ORDER.   21st. August. 1918.

1.   The Battalion will be prepared to move at half an hours notice from 8.0 a.m. to-morrow, 22nd. inst.
        The role of the 18th. Division is to form a defensive flank EAST of ALBERT.   The 53rd. Brigade is in Reserve.

2.   In the event of an enemy withdrawal, the 53rd. Brigade will form the Advanced Guard. This force will be devided into Van-Guard, Main Guard and two Flank Guards. The Advance will be made by a series of bounds.

3.   Each man will carry one day's rations and unconsumed portion of the day's ration in addition to the Iron Ration.   50% will also carry one extra Water-bottle filled.
        Each Rifleman will carry either a Pick or Shovel in the proportion of 4 Shovels to one Pick.
        2 Hand Wire Cutters per platoon will be carried.
        20 Lewis Gun Magazines per gun will be carried on the men of the Lewis Gun Sections as specially arranged. Lewis Gun teams will consist of 1 Leader and 5 Men, who will carry one bandolier S.A.A. each.
        16 Cup Dischargers per Company and 16 No.36 Grenades per platoon, also 100 No.23 Grenades per Company will be carried.
        1 Tin Disc for signalling to Contact Aeroplanes will be carried by each man.
        5 Very Light Pistols per Company and 1 packet of V.P.A, White, per Pistol will be carried.
        Each Company will take one bicycle.   "D" Company will draw a bicycle from Battalion Headquarter Runners for this purpose.

4.   On the Battalion moving, O.C. "B" and "D" Coys., will each detail one man to report to Quartermaster for Battalion Kit Dump Guard, No.20 Billet, WARLOY.

5.   2/Lieut. R.P. WOODYEAR. M.C., and one cyclist runner will report to Brigade Headquarters at D.4.c.2.3. at 10.0 a.m. 22nd. inst.

6.   One water cart will be available between 7.0 a.m. and 8.0 a.m. 22nd. inst. for filling water-bottles.
        O.C. Coys. will ensure that all water-bottles are filled before moving off.

7.   Officers' Valises and men's Overcoats and spare kits will be dumped at Company Headquarters by 6.30 a.m. 22nd. inst.

        A Lewis Gun Limber per Company will report to each Company to-night and will be loaded by 6.30 a.m., 22nd. inst.

8.   Reveille on 22nd. inst., will be at 5.0 a.m., Breakfasts 7.0 a.m. The Dump mentioned in para. 7 will be made after Reveille.

                                        (Signed:-) L.F.S. SPALDING,
                                                   Captain and Adjutant,
                                        7th. Battalion Royal West Kent Regiment.

Issued at......6.15. p.m.

          Copy No. 1. C.O.   No.6. O.C. "C" Coy
           "   " 2. Adjt.   " 7. O.C. "D" "
           "   " 3. O.C. "H.Q." Coy.   " 8. Q.M.
           "   " 4. O.C. "A"   "   " 9. T.O.
           "   " 5. O.C. "B"   "   " 10. R.S.M.

7th Battalion Royal West Kent Regiment.

SECRET.   22nd August 1918.

OPERATION ORDER No. 36.

The 53rd. Inf. Bde. will attack to-morrow 23rd. inst., objective W.30.b.5.7. to W.30.d.8.4. to a point running about E.6.a.8.5.

The objective of the Battalion is W.30.b.8.7. to W.30.d.8.4. BECOURT - ALBERT Road inclusive.

"A" Coy on the left, "B" Coy on the right. The dividing line between these Coys will be at W.30.b.8.0.

"C" Coy is in support, with its objective running from W.30.a.8.4. to W.30.d.4.4.

"D" Coy is in Reserve with its objective running North of SHAMROCK TREE at W.30.c.5.2.

Forming up position will be astride the BECOURT-ALBERT Road on Light Railway at W.29.c. and E.5.a.

"A" Coy position will be from 250 yds North of the road to the road.

"B" Coy position will be from the road to 250 yds South.

"C" Coy behind "A" Coy and as close as possible. "D" Coy immediately behind "C" Coy.

"B" Coy will advance with its left flank on BECOURT-ALBERT Road as far as SHAMROCK TREE at W.30.c.5.2. They will then cross the road until their right flank rests on it.

"A" Coy will advance with their right flank on the road as far as SHAMROCK TREE and will then advance with their right conforming to "B" Coy's left flank.

The leading Coys must advance from their forming up positions as far as possible before ZERO hour.

All Coys will advance in waves of platoons. Coys will consolidate in depth and will use the enemy's trenches unless necessary. They will dig slits in front or in rear.

If front line Coys. cannot form up in front of light railway, they will commence to advance 20 minutes before ZERO in order to reach barrage.

"C" Coy. will act as Counter-Attack Coy. without awaiting orders from Bn. H.Q.   "D" Coy. will not move without orders from Bn. H.Q.

ZERO hour 4.45 a.m.

The Battalion will leave its present position at 10.55 p.m. to-day marching by platoons at 100 yards distance in the following order :-   "A", "B", "C", "D" and "H.Q." Coy.

7th. Battn. "Queens" will be on our left and 10th. Bn. Essex on the right.

(Signed:-) G.G.THOMSON, Lieut.
A/Adjutant,
VOVU.

7th. Battalion Royal West Kent Regiment.

NARRATIVE OF ATTACK ON 23rd. AUGUST, 1918.

Ref. Maps - 57.D. S.W. and 62.D.N.E.

On 22nd. August, 1918, the 7th. Battalion Royal West Kent Regiment was ordered to attack on the morning of 23rd., in conjunction with 10th. Battalion ESSEX Regiment on right and 7th. Battalion "QUEEN'S" Regiment on left.

The attack was made with tanks under a barrage.

The assembly positions allotted were as follows:-

"A" Company along light railway in W.29.c. immediately NORTH of the ALBERT -- BECOURT Road.
"B" Company along light railway in E.5.a. immediately SOUTH and including ALBERT -- BECOURT Road.
"C" Company behind "B" Company in E.5.a.
"D" Company behind "A" Company in W.29.c.

The objective of the Battalion was a line running NORTH from the copse at W.30.d.9.5. to a point in the enemy's trenches at W.30.b.5.6.

Coys., were allotted the following objectives :-

"A" Company from W.30.b.5.6. to W.30.b.7.1.
"B" Company from W.30.b.7.1. to W.30.d.9.5.
"C" Company in elements of trenches from W.30.d.1.9. to W.30.d.4.5. where they would be in support and act as counter-attack Company.
"D" Company to dig in on a line running NORTH from SHAMROCK TREE at W.30.c.4.2. to W.30.c.4.8. where they would be in reserve.

At 4.45 a.m. on the 23rd. August, 1918, the barrage opened and the Battalion advanced in lines of sections behind the tanks. The enemy's artillery which had been active on our forming up positions during the night, immediately opened, but their barrage fell behind the attacking troops and caused very few casualties. Except for the enemy's Machine Guns, there was very little resistance and the objective was reached and the line consolidated. During the day the enemy shelled our new positions and kept up persistent Machine Gun fire, but no counter-attack developed.

This attack was followed by one which took place at 1.0 a.m. on the 24th. August, 1918.

Major,
Commanding 7th. Battalion Royal West Kent Regiment..

APP 131

7th. Battalion Royal West Kent Regiment.

NARRATIVE OF ATTACK ON 24th. AUGUST, 1918.

Ref. Maps - 57.D. S.E. and 62.D. N.E.

On 23rd. August, 1918, the 7th. Battalion Royal West Kent Regiment, less two Coys., was ordered to take part in an attack in conjunction with the other Battalions of the Brigade.

The assembly positions allotted were as follows :-
"C" Company in branch from W.30.b.6.4. to W.30.b.7.2.
"D" Company along banks in W.30.b.4.3.

The objective of the Battalion was to form a flank facing SOUTH along enemy C.T. from W.30.b.7.4. to X.25.b.7.8. joining up with the 8th. Battalion Royal Berks Regiment on the left

At 1.0 a.m. on the 24th. August, 1918 the barrage opened and the two Coys., advanced along the line of the two C.Ts. running through W.30.b. X.25.a. to X.19.d. Two Platoons advanced between the two trenches and a platoon with two of its sections on either side, advanced up each of the C.Ts. until the objective was reached. The remaining two platoons followed behind and established posts facing SOUTH along the Southern communication trench.

The position was gained without any serious opposition and immediately the line had been established, patrols were sent out to exploit in the direction of BECOURT WOOD. Eventually posts were established on the northern edge of the WOOD at X.25.b.3.5. and X.25.b.8.5. and along the western edge at X.25.c.8.5. and X.25.b.0.1.

A strong fighting patrol was sent out during the day towards the eastern side of BECOURT WOOD and after clearing the WOOD and CHATEAU, posts were established on the eastern outskirts of the WOOD, linking up with posts of the 10th. Battalion ESSEX Regt., on the right and 8th. Battalion Royal BERKS Regiment on the left.

Captain,
7th. Battalion Royal West Kent Regiment.

SECRET (W) APP. 132

WARNING ORDER
7th Bn. Royal West Kent Regt.

26th August 1916

1. The Battn. will move at 5.0 p.m. to-day to vicinity of BECOURT

2. "A" & "C" Coys will move with their Cookers on receipt of this order to Bn H.Q.

3. New Battle Surplus will be left behind when Battn. moves & proceed to HENENCOURT. On arrival of old Battle Surplus BAND and men for LEAVE will accompany them.

4. If the old Battle Surplus have not returned before the Battn. moves off 2/Lieut Woolley will

2

4 (Contd)
remain to guide them to Batt.

5 Lewis Gun Limbers will accompany Coys.
Batt. Stores Limber will follow
H.Q. Coy

6 Batt. will form up on track
WEST of Bn. H.Q. facing
SOUTH in the following order:-
    H.Q. Coy
    A
    B
    C
    D
at 4.35 p.m.

(Signed) L.F.S. SPALDING
Capt and Adjt
7th Bn Royal West Kent Regt

App. 132.A

7th. Battalion Royal West Kent Regiment.

NARRATIVE OF ATTACK ON 27th. AUGUST, 1918. - Ref.Map.Sheet.57.C. S.W.

-----------oOo-----------

On the evening of the 26th. August, 1918, the 7th. Batn. Royal West Kent Regiment moved forward to take up a new position in the vicinity of BECOURT. When passing Divisional H.Qrs., verbal orders were given to the Commanding Officer to attack the enemy the following morning in conjunction with the other Battalions of the Brigade.

The Battalion assembled along the sunken road running NORTH and SOUTH through S.21.d. on a one company frontage, with the 8th.R.F's. Regt. on the left and the 10th.R.Essex Regt. in support. "D" Coy. were in front with the other Coys. behind in the following order :-
"D", "A", "B" and "C" Coys.

The objective of the Battalion was to form a Flank facing SOUTH by advancing through BERNAFAY WOOD from the NORTH, and establishing a line 300m. of the WOOD from S.28.d.3.1. running in an EASTERLY direction to a point SOUTH of TRONES WOOD at S.29.d.9.5. where it would link up with the 8th. Batt. Royal Berks Regt.

At 4.55 a.m. the barrage opened, and the Battalion advanced along the line of the road running EAST through S.22.c & d. and 23.c & d., which the front Coy. reached the WESTERN edge of TRONES WOOD. The second Coy. established themselves along the line of HULCH and EDEN JEAN when desperately to advance. "C" Coy. also took up through the WOOD when the barrage lifted. "B" Coy. also took up a position facing SOUTH with the intention of advancing South- WARDS through the WOOD between BERNAFAY and TRONES WOOD at a Coy. of the 8th. R.B. Essex Regt. on his left who were to clear through the WOOD.

Up to this point the advance had been carried out with very little resistance on our front, but owing to LONGUEVAL and DELVILLE WOOD still being in the enemy's hands the 8th.Batt. R.BERKS Regt., were unable to make such good progress, and their left flank was held up.

The barrage was timed to lift southwards at 6.21 a.m. but it was considerably later before it moved on and "A" and "D" Coys. had to wait in their positions until it did so.

When the second phase of the attack started, "B" Company were able to make rapid progress between the two woods but "A" Coy. met with considerable opposition in BERNAFAY WOOD which however they eventually cleared and established their line 300 yards SOUTH of the WOOD linking up with "D" Coy. on their left. "D" Company were unable to get in touch with the Royal Berks.

"B" Coy. meanwhile, had been working forward to get into position at S.23.c. but they met with considerable Machine Gun fire from guns which had not been mopped up in S.28.a. and S.22.c. and during the morning a considerable amount of Machine Gunning and Sniping came from the NORTH of the road running through S.22.c & d. and 23.c & d.

At 6.40 a.m. a message was received from the C.O. of the 8th. Bn. Royal Berks Regt., that the enemy were in large numbers at the Sugar Refinery in S.24.b.0.9. and had advanced from there to about S.24.c.1.7. Also that there were swarms of the enemy in LONGUEVAL and DELVILLE WOOD.

At 8.0 a.m. the enemy counter-attacked the junction of Royal Berks and Royal West Kents and drove the line in to the EASTERN edge of BERNAFAY WOOD. "A" Coy. hung on to their positions and threw back a defensive flank to link up with "D" Coy. Touch had been found with the 12th. Division on the right.

NARRATIVE OF ATTACK ON 27th. August, 1918. (continued).

The line was thinly held and 2 Coys. of the 10th. Bttn. Essex Regiment came up in close support.

"B" Company by now had been placed at the disposal of the C.O. of the 8th. Battn. Royal Berks Regiment, and had taken up a position along the line of the sunken road running from S.23.c.3.9. to S.23.c.0.5.

An attack was ordered to take place at 7.0 p.m. by the Commanding Officer of the 8th. Royal Berks Regiment to re-establish the line EAST of TRONES WOOD and SOUTH of the light railway with the help of a Company of the 10th. Battn. Essex Regt., "D" Coy. of the R.W.Kent Regiment had to follow the attacking troops and re-establish their original line facing SOUTH. This attack was successfully carried out and the whole of the objective gained.

The following morning the 12th. Division attacked on our right and "A" Company exploited and formed a liaison post 100 yards WEST of MALTZ HORN FARM with this Division.

Major,
Commanding 7th. Battalion Royal West Kent Regiment.

SECRET.   28th August 1918.
                           APP 133

Operation Order No 6.

The Battalion will be relieved by the 6th NORTHAMPTINSHIRE REGT with the exception of "B" Coy. who will be relieved by the 2nd BEDFORDSHIRE REGT. "A" Coy. R.W.K. will be relieved by 1 Platoon of "B" Coy. NORTHANTS REGT. "D" Coy. will be relieved by "D" Coy 6th NORTHANTS R
"C"   "   "   "   "   " "C"   "   "   "   "
"B"   "   "   "   "   " "B"   " 2nd BEDFORDS

Guides:-
"A" Coy. will send 1 guide to report to R. BERKS H.Q. at 7.0 p.m.
"B" Coy will send guides to the proportion of 1 per platoon & 1 per Coy H.Q. to R. BERKS H.Q at 7.0 p.m.
"C" & D Coys. will send guides to the same proportions to report to Adjutant in the SUNKEN ROAD, WEST of BERNAFAY WOOD at S.28.b.5.6 at 7.0 p.m.
O.C "C" Coys will detail an Officer to report to Adjutant at 7.0 pm in the

2

SUNKEN ROAD

On completion of relief Coys will move independently to the SUPPORT Position in the vicinity of MONTAUBAN via the QUARRY in S.a.d.9.5. where they will be met by guides who will lead them into their new position. Coys will carry out with them all empty petrol tins, Lewis Gun drums and S.O.S. Rockets.

Completion of relief will be notified by runners to the new Bn H.Q in the SUNKEN Road near S.26.b.5.6. One of the guides who knows the position should be used for this purpose.

Arrival in new position will be notified to Bn H.Q. which will probably be known to the guides who met you at QUARRY.

(Signed) G.G THOMPSON Lieut
for Captain Adjutant,
V.O.V.U.

SECRET.   29-5-18.

                                   APP 134

                Operation Order No 44

The Battalion will move to-night to
garrison positions about T.27.a. & c. & T.26.
Order of march :-
        'C' 'B' 'A' 'D' & H.Q. Coys.
Head of Column will fall in
on Sunken Road at S.25.c.2.7 at
7-45 p.m.
Coys will move with 100 yards
Intervals between Coys & 50 yards
between Platoons.
ROUTE : MONTAUBAN - TRONES WOOD
GUILLEMONT ROAD
All Ranks to be warned about
booby traps and usual precautions
to be taken with all Water.

                        (Signed -) W.A. SHEARING
                                 for Capt & ADJT

SECRET   30/8/16

Operation Order No 50

1. The Bn will move today to positions about line of WEDGE WOOD - GINCHY Rd. East of GUILLEMONT and will hold as permanent garrison the line T27 a 7.7 to T21 c 4.7.

The Bn will be disposed of as under:-
A Coy. in Trenches about T26 a & c
B   "   "   "   "   T27 c
C   "   "   "   "   T21 c & 27 b.
D   "   East of Road Running N & S through T26 a & c

Bn HQ will be about T26 c 0.9.

If the tactical situation demands of it 'B' Coy will occupy Trench running through T27 d.

'A' Coy will be counter attack Coy
The 16 Bn Essex Regt will be on the left and 47th Divn on right.

2. Bn will move at 1.30 p.m.
Order of March:-
   C. B. A. D. HQ Coys.

Intervals of 100 yds between platoons will be maintained. Connecting files to be used.

2

L.G's and magazines will be
carried on the mus

Coy will report when in position
and locations of Lay L.G.

W A SHEARING 2/Lt
for Capt + Adjt
ymB RW Kent R

WAR DIARY of INTELLIGENCE SUMMARY.

(Erase heading not required.)

Army Form C. 2118.

Place	Date	Hour	Summary of Events and Information	Remarks and references to Appendices
In the Line.	1-9-18.	19.00	Battalion attached to 55th Inf. Bde; attacked and captured SAILLY=SAILLISEL. Slight opposition. Advance commenced 19.00; objective reached and consolidated by 22.00	App. 136 App. 137
	2-9-18.		Enemy counter-attacked under M.G. barrage, but were driven off. Heavy hostile shelling and fire from snipers.	
	3-9-18.		Battn. followed retiring enemy and finally halted in Support to other Battns of Bde., in U.21.b. and 21.a. (Sheet 57.C.S.W. and 62.C.NW.)	
	4-9-18.		Battn. moved back to vicinity of MONTAUBAN.	
nr.MONTAUBAN.	5-9-18. to 9-9-18.		Battalion resting and re-organising.	
	10-9-18. to 14-9-18.		Battalion Training and refitting.	App. 138
	15-9-18.		Warning Order to move to Line on 16th.	
	16-9-18.		Battalion proceeded by 'Bus and march route to vicinity of AIZECOURT-LE-BAS	
AIZECOURT-LE-BAS	17-9-18.		Battalion advanced and captured Western outskirts of RONSSOY. Bn. withdrew in the evening and moved to ST.EMILIE.	App. 139 App. 140 App. 141
ST.EMILIE.	18-9-18.		Orders received to attack at 11.0 am on 19th.	
LINE.	19-9-18.		"C" Coy reached junction of BIRD TRENCH and ST.PATRICK's TRENCH. Other objectives were not taken.	
	20-9-18.		"D" Coy patrolled forward to ZEBRA POST and BRAYTON POST. Forward Coys Relieved in evening by troops of 12th Divn. and 53 Bde.M.G.C., and withdrew to RONSSOY and LEMPIRE.	
	21-9-18.		"D" Coy plus R.E.platoon successfully attacked at 5.0 a.m. and consolidated on a line about 300 yds North of SART FARM. Patrol unsuccessfully attempted to take EGG POST.	App. 142 App. 143
	22-9-18.		"B" and "C" Coys occupied SART FARM without molestation by enemy in daylight. Patrols to make good EGG POST and S.E. half of GRAFTON TRENCH met with very strong opposition and did not gain their objectives, although a patrol under 2/Lt.A.F.NEILL made three separate very determined attacks on EGG POST during the night. Bn. relieved by 8th R.Berks Rgt in SART FARM.	
	23-9-18.		Three Coys withdrawn to RONSSOY before daylight and remained there during the day.	
	24-9-18.		"A" Coy, with "B" Coy in support unsuccessfully attacked EGG POST and TAG SUPPORT. A small detachment under 2/Lt.A.B.CULLERNE established itself in a small trench about 400 yds South	

Army Form C. 2118.

WAR DIARY
or
INTELLIGENCE SUMMARY.
(Erase heading not required.)

Instructions regarding War Diaries and Intelligence Summaries are contained in F. S. Regs., Part II. and the Staff Manual respectively. Title pages will be prepared in manuscript.

Place	Date	Hour	Summary of Events and Information	Remarks and references to Appendices
LINE.	24-9-18.		of EGG POST. Coys were withdrawn to RONSSOY with exception of the detachment previously mentioned, which could not be relieved in daylight.	App. 144
	25-9-18.		Battn. moved to GURLU WOOD where it remained for the night.	App. 145
GURLU WOOD.	26-9-18.		Battn. marched to B.15.c. and d., EAST of MAUREPAS.	
MAUREPAS.	27-9-18.		Battn. resting and refitting.	
	28-9-18.		Battn. resting and re-organising. During afternoon marched to NURLU.	App. 146
NURLU.	29-9-18.		Battn. moved to Area E.4. East of GUYENCOURT.	App. 147
	30-9-18.		Battn. relieved 6th Battn. Queens Regt. in reserve in area X.28.b. and d.	App. 148

CASUALTIES :-

	Killed	Wounded	Missing
Officers	4	3	-
O.R.	42	184	19

Officer Casualties during month

```
Captain T.L.TANNER........   Killed in Action 18-9-18
2/Lieut. P.J.PETER.........  Killed in Action 19-9-18
2/Lieut. J.S.LARKEN........  Killed in Action 22-9-18.
Lieut. P. STEVENS..........  Killed in Action 23-9-18.
Lieut. P.D.GAUSDEN.........  Wounded in Action. 19-9-18.
2/Lieut. M. J.CLAPHAM......  Wounded in Action. 19-9-18.
2/Lieut. E.C.ROBERTSON.....  Wounded in Action 24-9-18.
2/Lieut J.COXON............  Sick to England. 2-9-18.
2/Lieut. G.A.BISHOP........  Sick to England 3-9-18.
Lieut. Ll.JONES............  To 53rd. T.M.B., 8-9-18.
Major A.E.PHILLIPS.........  To Commd. Vth Corps Cyclist Battn., 15-9-18
```

Army Form C. 2118.

WAR DIARY
or
INTELLIGENCE SUMMARY.
(Erase heading not required.)

Summary of Events and Information

Officer Casualties during Month (Contd.)
Major S.W.WARR.......... To 8th Battn. R.Berks Rgt. 19-9-18.
Lieut. R.P.WOODYEAR. MC.... To England for Duty with R.A.F., 25-9-18.

Officers joined during Month.
Lieut. A.V.D.MORLEY. MC... Rejoined 22-9-18.

HONOURS & AWARDS.
Bar to the MILITARY CROSS................... Capt. A.V.McDONALD.M.C.
  Lieut. H.J.M.HARRIS.M.C.
The MILITARY CROSS......................... Lieut. G.G.THOMSON.
The DISTINGUISHED CONDUCT MEDAL............ 24797. Sgt. G.H.Daniels.
Second Bar to MILITARY MEDAL............... 10421. Pte. F.Stacey M.M.
Bar to MILITARY MEDAL...................... 19122. C.S.M., L.Green. M.M.
  21003. Sgt. A.Jackson M.M.
The MILITARY MEDAL......................... 14614. Pte. W. Webberley.
  21536. Pte. M.Kelly.
  29963. Pte. L.Batchelor.
  21501. L/Sgt. M.J.Sterry.
  265663 Sgt. A.J.Gearing.
  29991. Pte. A.Wakefield.
  26369. L/C. C.Jones.
  21433. L/C. E.Humphries.

———————oOo———————

4th October 1918.

Major

Commdg. 7th Battalion Royal West Kent Regt.

NARRATIVE OF ATTACK ON 1ST. SEPTEMBER, 1918.

Ref. Maps. 57.C.-S.W. and 62.C.-N.W.
---oOo---

On the 1st. of September, 1918, the 7th. Battalion Royal West Kent Regiment, whilst attached to the 55th. Infantry Brigade, was ordered to attack and capture the village of SAILLISEL in conjunction with 38th. Division who were to attack SAILY SAILLISEL at the same time.

When the order was received, the Battalion was stationed near advanced Brigade Headquarters at T.26.c., and as the attack was to take place in the evening, it was necessary to move up to the jumping off positions in daylight. This was carried out without a casualty in spite of the fact that the enemy had observation from balloons practically the whole time. The route taken was via the valley in B.2.3. & 4., thence in artillery formation to PRIEZ FARM in B.6.a. and from there to the forming up position which was approximately the front line running from U.19.b.8.8. in a SOUTH-EASTERLY direction to U.20.c.9.1. "B" Coy. on the left and "C" Coy. on the right made the attack with "A" Coy. in Support and "D" Coy. in Reserve.

"B" Coys. objective was the NORTH-EAST edge of the village from U.8.d.0.0. to U.15.a.0.4. "C" Coys. objective was from U.15.a.0.4. to U.15.a.7.0., thence running SOUTH-WEST to U.15.c.2.0.

"A" Coy. was made responsible for filling up any gap between "C" Coys. right and the 7th. Battn. The BUFFS who were to swing round and establish a line along the NORTH-WEST edge of ST. PIERRE VAAST WOOD from U.15.c.2.0. to U.20.d.0.0., after the attacking troops had gone through.

"D" Coy. were to establish themselves in trenches in U.14.c.

Previous to ZERO hour and whilst the Coys. were forming up, the enemy kept up a harrassing Machine Gun fire.

At 7.0 p.m. the barrage opened and the Battalion advanced, but met very little opposition. Except for a few snipers and Machine Gunners, there were scarcely any of the enemy in SAILLISEL. The objective was reached and consolidated by 10.0 p.m.

At 6.0 a.m. on the 2nd. September, 1918, the enemy counter-attacked under a Machine Gun barrage but were driven off. During the day our new positions were heavily shelled with guns of all calibres and snipers were particularly active.

During the night 2nd./3rd. September, 1918, villages were burning in front of our lines and on the morning of the 3rd., patrols reported that the enemy had apparently retired. In conjunction with units on our left and right, the Battalion followed up and finally halted in Support to the other Battalions of the Brigade in U.21.b. and 21.a.

Major,
Commanding 7th. Battalion Royal West Kent Regiment.

NARRATIVE OF ATTACK ON 1ST. SEPTEMBER, 1918.

Ref. Maps. 57.C.-S.W. and 62.C.-N.W.

---oOo---

On the 1st. of September, 1918, the 7th. Battalion Royal West Kent Regiment, whilst attached to the 55th. Infantry Brigade, was ordered to attack and capture the village of SAILLISEL in conjunction with 38th. Division who were to attack SAILLY SAILLISEL at the same time.

When the order was received, the battalion was stationed near advanced Brigade Headquarters at T.26.c., and as the attack was to take place in the evening, it was necessary to move up to the jumping off positions in daylight. This was carried out without a casualty in spite of the fact that the enemy had observation from balloons practically the whole time. The route taken was via the valley in B.2,3, & 4., thence in artillery formation to PRIEZ FARM in B.6.a. and from there to the forming up position which was approximately the front line running from U.19.b.8.0. in a SOUTH-EASTERLY direction to U.20.c.9.1. "B" Coy. on the left and "C" Coy. on the right made the attack with "A" Coy. in Support and "D" Coy. in Reserve.

"B" Coys. objective was the NORTH-EAST edge of the village from U.8.d.0.0. to U.15.a.0.4. "C" Coys. objective was from U.15.a.0.4. to U.15.a.7.0., thence running SOUTH-WEST to U.15.c.2.0.

"A" Coy. was made responsible for filling up any gap between "C" Coys. right and the 7th. Battn. The BUFFS who were to swing round and establish a line along the NORTH-WEST edge of ST. PIERRE VAAST WOOD from U.15.c.2.0. to U.20.d.0.0., after the attacking troops had gone through.

"D" Coy. were to establish themselves in trenches in U.14.c.

Previous to ZERO hour and whilst the Coys. were forming up, the enemy kept up a harrassing Machine Gun fire.

At 7.0 p.m. the barrage opened and the Battalion advanced, but met very little opposition. Except for a few snipers and Machine Gunners, there were scarcely any of the enemy in SAILLISEL. The objective was reached and consolidated by 10.0 p.m.

At 6.0 a.m. on the 2nd. September, 1918, the enemy counter-attacked under a Machine Gun barrage but were driven off. During the day our new positions were heavily shelled with guns of all calibres and snipers were particularly active.

During the night 2nd./3rd. September, 1918, villages were burning in front of our lines and on the morning of the 3rd., patrols reported that the enemy had apparently retired. In conjunction with units on our left and right, the Battalion followed up and finally halted in Support to the other Battalions of the Brigade in U.21.b. and 21.a.

Major,
Commanding 7th. Battalion Royal West Kent Regiment.

SECRET. Copy No........

7th. Battalion Royal West Kent Regiment.

OPERATION ORDER NO.54.

15th. September, 1918.

1. The Battalion less Battle Surplus will move forward to-morrow, 16th. September, 1918. It will proceed by route march to the Embussing Point on main road at LEUZE WOOD, which is to be reached by 10.0 a.m. (T.21.c.1.4.)
   On the march from debussing point to billets, Coys. will keep 200 yards distance. If enemy aircraft are encountered, troops will fall out on side of the road and remain still. THEY WILL NOT LOOK UP.

2. The Battalion will form up on the road opposite 53rd. Inf. Brigade Headquarters in column of route facing NORTH at 8.15 a.m.
   Order of March :- Headquarters, "A" Coy., "B" Coy., "C" Coy., and "D" Coy.
   Dress :- Fighting Order.
   Lewis Guns will be carried on Limbers.
   Lewis Gun Magazines will be carried.
   100 yards distance will be maintained between Coys.

3. Transport will move separately under Brigade Orders.

4. Lieut. G.G.THOMSON and 1 N.C.O. from each Coy. will proceed to the embussing point at 7.30 a.m. The party will report at Battalion Headquarters at 7.20 a.m.

Issued at 11.55 p.m.

(Signed:-) L.F.S.SPALDING,
Captain and Adjutant,
7th. Battalion Royal West Kent Regiment.

7th Battalion Royal West Kent Regiment.

NARRATIVE OF THE OPERATIONS FROM 17th SEPT. to 24th SEPT. 1918

17-9-18. The Battalion being at AIZECOURT-LE-BAS marched to forming-up positions East of ST. EMILIE. Dispositions:- Front line "A" Coy on left, "D" Coy on Right, "C" Coy in Support in Centre, "B" Coy in rear of "C" Coy and behind "A" Coy.

"A" Coy were given as Objective, a line running North and South about 300 yds East of the CHURCH in RONSSOY VILLAGE through the CEMETERY, bounded by the two main roads.
"D" Coy were to continue this line Southwards for about 200 yds.
"C" Coy were to mop-up and make good RONSSOY WOOD.
"B" Coy were to leave two posts on left flank, one at jumping-off point, and one about 300 yds South of the N.W. corner of RONSSOY WOOD. The remainder of the Coy were to establish themselves in the trench West of the South portion of RONSSOY WOOD.

These positions were eventually gained.

18-9-18. Coys were in position by 3.30 a.m. Battn. H.Q. were established in trench about 100 yds behind "B" Coy at 4.0 a.m. The line to Brigade was cut by enemy shells.

When the barrage opened at 5.20 a.m., the mist was so heavy that it was impossible to see more than a few yards ahead.

The enemy barrage was very thin, and the Battn. experienced very few casualties during the advance. Captn. T.L. TANNER, Commandng "C" Coy was killed very early.

Owing to mist, Coys lost the Barrage soon after the start, and to some extent their direction also; they arrived at South end of RONSSOY WOOD.

"A" and "D" Coys were through RONSSOY WOOD at 7.20 a.m., and at 9.0 were found established on their objectives.

Battn. H.Q. had followed up "B" Coy, but in the mist passed them and arrived at RONSSOY WOOD with the front line Coys. After the Coys were re-organised for further advance Battn. H.Q. were established in same trench with "B" Coy, and later in the day moved back to a quarry about 400 yds West of it.

The Battn were withdrawn in the evening to ST. EMILIE. Owing to the runner carrying the Order to "A" and "B" Coys being hit, these two Coys did not arrive until about midnight.

Late in the evening Orders were received to attack at 11.0 a.m., the next morning, 19th Sept.

19-9-18. At 10.45 a.m., "C", "B" and "A" Coys were in position on the line of the road running South East and North West through LEMPIRE, "D" Coy in Reserve in trench on North edge of RONSSOY WOOD, Battn. H.Q. F.15.d.4.7. (Sheet 62.C.NE.) The telephone line to Bde. H.Q. was not through.

8th R.BERKS RGT were to take the first objective, and 7th R.W. KENT RGT to go through and take the second.
"C" Coy ordered to take ST. PATRICK's AVENUE and consolidate.
"B" Coy ordered to take ZEBRA POST.
"A" Coy ordered to take BRAETON POST.

Barrage opened at 11.0 a.m.
At 12.20 p.m., O.C., 8th R.BERKS RGT reported his Right Coy on objective and that R.W. KENT Coy had gone through.

(2.)

8th R.BERKS RGT were held up by heavy M.G. fire. "B" and "A" Coys, R.W.KENT RGT supporting behind DOSE TRENCH.

At 1.30 p.m., enemy were still in YAK POST; 8th R.BERKS established in trench juncture at F.10.a.6.3.

At 1.30 p.m., "C" Coy R.W.KENT RGT commenced to bomb up ST.PATRICK'S TRENCH and HOLLOW ROAD parallel with it as far as F.10.a.8.9.

At 3.0 p.m. Bn.H.Q. moved to dug-out at F.15.d.7.6.

"C" Coy reached juncture of BIRD TRENCH and ST.PATRICKS TRENCH at about 6.0 p.m.
ZEBRA POST was never reached, but YAK POST was mistaken for ZEBRA by both 8th R.BERKS Rgt. and 7th R.W.KENT Rgt.
At 7.40 p.m., S.O.S. signal was sent up on Corps front, barrage replied; there was no counter attack on Bn. front.
At 8. p.m. "A" Coy was withdrawn to RONSSOY.
"B" Coy to RIDGE RESERVE South, at about F.15.a.0.8.
"C" Coy to SUNKEN ROAD at F.10.c.3.4.

20-9-18.   At 4.10 a.m., "D" Coy were ordered to patrol forward to ZEBRA POST and BRAETON POST, and "B" Coy were ordered to relieve 8th R.BERKS Rgt in ZEBRA POST.

Patrolling continued throughout the day; BIRD TRENCH was reached, but not BRAETON POST.
Reports as to our and enemy positions throughout the day were conflicting, our patrols being fired on from positions reported to be in hands of 12th Divn, chiefly HORSE POST and BRAETON POST.

In the evening, troops of the 12th Divn. took over all forward positions held by the Battn. except YAK POST which was relieved by 53rd. Bde. M.G.Corps troops, and Coys were withdrawn to RONSSOY and LEMPIRE.

Orders were received about 10.0 p.m. for one Coy to take part in an attack at 5.40 a.m. the next morning. The task was allotted to "D" Coy., to whom were attached the R.E. platoon found by the Battn.
The attack was to be carried out in two phases. The first by the R.W.KENT Rgt with SART FARM as objective, and the second by the 10th ESSEX Rgt with THE KNOLL as objective.
Seven tanks co-operated, and there was a creeping barrage for both phases.
One Coy 8th R.BERKS Rgt was attached to the 7th R.W.KENT Rgt. as Support Coy., but was not called upon.

21-9-18.   At 5.0 a.m. "D" Coy were on their jumping-off line, and barrage opened at 5.40 a.m.
"D" Coy reached their objective successfully ad consolidated on a line about 300 yds North of SART FARM.
A patrol was sent forward to take EGG POST, but were unable to take it.
10th ESSEX Rgt. were fired at from behind, probably from HORSE POST; they suffered heavily and were unable to reach their objective. Some fell back on SART FARM.
"D" Coy were in touch with NORTHANTS Rgt at DOLEFUL POST.

Patrols were sent up POMPONIUS LANE and FLEECEALL LANE; they were fired on from EGG POST and had to withdraw.
A supply of bombs and S.A.A. was got up to SART FARM during the afternoon.

(3.)

About 9.0 p.m., Orders were received that one Coy 7th R.W.KENT Rgt were to be lent to 8th R.BERKS Rgt., for support in an attack to be carried out at 12.15 a.m. 22nd. Owing to the loss of DOLEFUL POST during the night this attack did not develop, and "A" Coy returned to the Battn., early on 22nd.

22-9-18.
The Coys at RONSSOY "Stood-to" at dawn, in anticipation of a counter-attack which did not develop, and they "Stood-down" at 7.0 a.m.

The men of the R.E. Platoon attached to "D" Coy were dribbled out of the line at about 11.0 a.m., and returned to their billets. Bde reported at 4.0 p.m. that 12th Divn. had occupied BRAFTON POST and were working Southwards. The Battn was ordered to carry out operations with a view to establishing EGG POST - T.11.a.7.6. line. At 4.50 p.m. a report was received from Bde that 12th Divn that 200 enemy had retired from TOMBOIS FARM under cover of heavy barrage, and ordering co-operation with 12th Divn., who were moving on TOMBOIS FARM.

"D" Coy were at once informed and ordered to push out strong patrol to meet 12th Divn along SART LANE to TOMBOIS FARM.

"C" and "B" Coys were ordered to proceed at once to SART FARM with orders to push right through towards THE KNOLL and capture it if possible. The action taken was reported to Bde., and "A" Coy were brought up into close reserve.

At about 6. p.m. Bde ordered cancellation of this operation, which had already commenced. Coys had already reached SART FARM without molestation in daylight.

In accordance with instructions from Bde., "B" and "C" Coys were ordered to send out strong Officer's patrol each, - "B" Coy to make good EGG POST and South East half of GRAFTON TRENCH, and "C" Coy North West half of GRAFTON TRENCH (NOTE:- it was afterwards discovered that GRAFTON TRENCH did not exist on the ground although marked on map 62.C.N.E. Ed. 5A(local))

Patrols were unable to make good their objectives, and met with strong opposition. The patrol under 2/Lieut A.F.NEILL made three separate very determined attacks on EGG POST during the night, but were beaten off each time.

During the evening a report was received that the 12th Div. had established a block at T.11.a.9.5., and were patrolling towards TOMBOIS FARM.

During the night 8th R.BERKS Rgt relieved 7th R.W.KENT Rgt in SART FARM. During the relief, the enemy shelled very heavily, causing some casualties, and killing Lieut. P.STEVENS, Offr. Comdg. "D" Coy, 7th R.W.KENT Rgt., who had very gallantly captured and held this post in difficult circumstances.

Before leaving, blocks were established in POMPONIUS LANE and FLEECEALL LANE, and handed over to 8th R.BERKS Rgt.

Bde was informed at about 2.0 a.m., 23rd, that attempt to establish position on Ridge had failed.

23-9-18.
The three Coys were withdrawn to RONSSOY before daylight, and remained there during the day.

In the afternoon orders were received that the Battn would carry out an attack that evening., with a view to capturing EGG POST and EAG SUPPORT.

"A" Coy was detailed as assaulting Coy., with "B" Coy in close support and under orders of O.C. "A" Coy. The attack was arranged for 3.0 a.m. 24th, in conjunction with an attack by the 12th Divn on the Left on TOMBOIS FARM, and with a gas attack by the 55th Bde on the Right on ISLAND TRAVERSE which was to be followed by actual attack at 5.0 a.m.

24-9-18.
At 3.0 a.m. "A" Coy advanced, but met strong opposition. A detachment of "B" Coy under 2/Lieut. A.B.CULLERNE established itself in a small trench element about 400 yds South of EGG POST where 12 enemy and 3 machine guns were captured. When the main attack withdrew, this detachment remained at its post.

At 6.0 a.m. another attempt was made under cover of smoke barrage, which however, was not thick enough to be of much service.

(4.)

An attempt was made to approach up POMPONIUS LANE, but the Post was held too strongly with many machine guns, and the attacking force had again to fall back, leaving the small advanced post in position.

The Coys were then withdrawn to RONSSOY with the exception of the Post mentioned, which could not be relieved in daylight.

CASUALTIES :-

Officers.	Killed-	Capt. T.L.TANNER.	18-9-18.
		2/Lt.P.J.PETER.	19-9-18.
		Lieut.P.STEVENS.	23-9-18.
		2/Lt.J.S.LARKEN.	22-9-18.
	Wounded.	Lieut. P.D.GAUSDEN.	19-9-18.
		2/Lt. L.J.CLAPHAM.	19-9-18.
		2/Lt. E.C.ROBERTSON.	24-9-18.
Other Ranks.	Killed..................................		29.
	Wounded.................................		154.
	Missing.................................		18.

-------------------oOo-------------------

Commanding 7th Battn. Royal West Kent Regt.

Field.
4-10-18.

SECRET.   Copy No...12...

MOVEMENT ORDER.

7th. Battalion Royal West Kent Regiment.

28th. September, 1918.

APP 146

1. The Battalion will march to NURLU this afternoon. Order of march, "H.Q." "A" Coy. "B" Coy. BAND, "C" Coy. "D" Coy. Battle Surplus.

2. Surplus Kit will be dumped on sunken road WEST of Camp by 11.0 a.m. The Quartermaster will have it conveyed to dump at Brigade H.Q. Everything else will be transported to NURLU.
Officers' Valises will be dumped on sunken road by 1.0 p.m. Mess Boxes by 2.0 p.m., and will be collected by Mess Cart

3. Transport will follow the Battalion.

4. Exact hour of move will be notified later. It will be about 2.0 p.m.

Issued at... 10.15 a.m. ...

(Signed:-) L.F.S. SPALDING,
Captain and Adjutant,
7th Battalion Royal West Kent Regiment.

Army Form C. 2118.

WAR DIARY
or
INTELLIGENCE SUMMARY.
(Erase heading not required.)

Instructions regarding War Diaries and Intelligence Summaries are contained in F.S. Regs., Part II. and the Staff Manual respectively. Title pages will be prepared in manuscript.

Place	Date	Hour	Summary of Events and Information	Remarks and references to Appendices
LINE.	1-10-18.		Warning Order that Battalion would be relieved.	
"	1/2-10-18.		Battalion withdrawn to Area E.4, EAST of GUYENCOURT.	
"	2-10-18.		Battalion embussed at W.26.d., N.W. of GUYENCOURT and arrived in Billets in CARDONNETTE at 1900.	App.149.
CARDON- NETTE.	3/13-10-18.		Battalion in Billets at CARDONNETTE. Re-organisation and Training.	
"	14-10-18.		Warning Order received to be prepared to move by Tactical Train at 24 hours notice.	
"	15-10-18.		Training.	
"	16-10-18.		Training. Warning Order to move to VILLERS FAUCON Area to-morrow.	
"	17-10-18.		Entrained POULAINVILLE 1230, Detrained ROISEL 2230, arrived VILLERS FAUCON 2300.	App.150.
"	18-10-18.		Embussed VILLERS FAUCON 1300 and arrived PREMONT at 1800.	App.151.
"	19-10-18.		Battalion marched to MAUROIS: arrived 1800.	App.152.
"	20-10-18.		Battalion left MAUROIS 1745 and relieved 9th. Battn. Manchester Regiment in the Line.	App.153.
LINE.	21/22-10-18.		Holding Line.	
"	23-10-18.		Battalion attacked at 0120 and captured GARDEMILL, ERVILLERS WOOD FARM and CORBEAU. All objectives gained by 0500. Battalion in billets at CORBEAU for the night 23/24th. October.	App.154.
"	24-10-18.		Battalion moved at 1800 to vicinity of BOUSIES (F.27.d.5.2.).	App.154.a.
"	25-10-18.		Battalion in close support.	
"	26-10-18.		Battalion in close support; "A" and "C" Coys. attached to 8th. Battn. Royal Berks Regiment and attacked at 0100.	App.154.b.
"	27-10-18.		Battalion relieved 8th. Battn. Royal Berks Regt., in left sector of Brigade front.	App.155.
"	28-10-18.		Holding Line.	
"	29-10-18.		Battalion relieved by 8th. Battn. East Surrey Regt., and moved to billets in BOUSIES.	App.156.
BOUSIES.	30-10-18.		In billets.	
"	31-10-18.		Battalion left BOUSIES at 1800 and relieved 8th. Battn. East Surrey Regt. in left sector of Brigade front.	App.157.

Casualties.

	Killed.	Wounded.	Missing.
Officers.	1	3	—
O.R.	12	62 (Including 2 at duty.)	3.

Army Form C. 2118.

WAR DIARY
or
INTELLIGENCE SUMMARY.
(Erase heading not required.)

Instructions regarding War Diaries and Intelligence Summaries are contained in F. S. Regs., Part II. and the Staff Manual respectively. Title pages will be prepared in manuscript.

Place	Date	Hour	Summary of Events and Information	Remarks and references to Appendices
	OCTOBER, 1918.		**OFFICERS' JOINED DURING THE MONTH.**	
			Major. A.F.S.NORTHCOTE. Rejoined 3-10-18.	
			2/Lieut. T.S.LEEMING. Joined. 8-10-18.	
			2/Lieut. H.S.LEE. " 8-10-18.	
			2/Lieut. P.J.BOLTON. " 8-10-18.	
			Capt. R.D.MILLIGAN. " 9-10-18.	
			2/Lieut. E.V.TOZER. " 9-10-18.	
			2/Lieut. W.G.BARRETT. " 9-10-18.	
			2/Lieut. G.A.OWEN. " 9-10-18.	
			2/Lieut. A.H.OAKLEY. " 9-10-18.	
			2/Lieut. G.A.STAPLEY. " 9-10-18.	
			2/Lieut. C.F.BALDWIN. M.M. " 9-10-18.	
			2/Lieut. B.FULLER. " 11-10-18.	
			Lieut. R.J.KNIGHT. " 31-10-18.	
			OFFICERS' CASUALTIES DURING THE MONTH.	
			2/Lieut. R.J.DICKINSON. Sick to England, 18-10-18.	
			2/Lieut. A.B.CULLERNE. M.C. Killed, 23-10-18.	
			2/Lieut. R.B.L.HILL. Wounded 24-10-18.	
			2/Lieut. J.C.WOOLLEY. Wounded 26-10-18.	
			2/Lieut. H.S.LEE. Wounded 27-10-18.	

7th. Battalion Royal West Kent Regiment.

BATTLE NARRATIVE.

Map Ref:-
Sheet 57.B. 1/40,000.

At 0120 on 23rd. October, 1918, the 7th. Battalion Royal West Kent Regiment attacked as part of the 53rd. Brigade, with the 10th. Battalion Essex Regiment on their left and the 8th. Battalion Royal Berks Regiment in Second wave.

The objectives allotted to the Battalion were distributed as follows :-
GARDEMILL to "B" Coy.
ERVILLERS WOOD FARM AND CORBEAU to "D" Coy.
PRACTICE TRENCHES in L.19.d. and L.20.c., to "A" Coy. and the Battalions portion of the first objective, - ROAD from L.20.central to L.20.d.b.4., to "C" Coy.

The 20th. Battalion of the Manchester Regiment were on the right of the Battalion and were responsible for the line GARDEMILL - POMMEREUIL - and the continuation of the first objective.

About half-way from the forming up position to the first objective, the RICHMONT RIVER runs accross the line of advance and presented the most serious obstacle to the attack. Light wooden bridges were carried to assist in crossing this stream.

At 0040 the Coys. were on their forming up positions, and at 0120 the barrage opened.

At the RICHMONT STREAM, the enemy Trench Mortars at CORBEAU caused most of the casualties suffered by the Battalion; here 2/Lieut. A.B.CULLERNE was killed while helping his men accross the stream; the only Officer casualty suffered by the Battalion in the attack.

By 0500 all objectives had been made good with slight loss and about 400 prisoners taken.

Battalion Headquarters moved forward to CORBEAU where the Battalion was concentrated for the night 23/24th. October.

(Signed:-) L.P.S.SPALDING,
Captain and Adjutant,
7th. Battalion Royal West Kent Regiment.

7th. Battalion Royal West Kent Regiment.

BATTLE NARRATIVE.

APP. 158

Ref. Map:-
57.A. N.W. 1/20,000.

At 0815 on 4th. November, 1918, the 7th. Battalion Royal West Kent Regiment attacked as part of the 53rd. Brigade with the assistance of Tanks. The 54th. Brigade were on the right and the 2nd. Battalion Royal Welsh Fusiliers on the left.

The objectives allotted to the Battalion were distributed as follows:-
"B" Coy., E outskirts of HECQ in A.9.c.
"C" Coy., E outskirts of HECQ in A.6.b.
"D" Coy., ROAD running NORTH from ROUTE D'HECQ in A.9.b.
"A" Coy., TRACK running SOUTH in A.9.d. and astride ROUTE D'HECQ.

The Battalion formed up along the sunken road running NORTH and SOUTH in A.7.b. & d.

At 0810 the tanks were reported going into action and at 0815 hours the barrage opened and "C" and "D" Coys. advanced to the attack. The first resistance was met with in front of and in the sunken road in A.8.a. & c.

Two Platoons of each Coy. established themselves respectively at the CROSS ROADS in A.8.a. and sunken road in A.8.c., and mopped up the enemy in the areas round these points. The remaining two Platoons of "C" and "D" Coys. went forward to their final objectives but met with considerable opposition in the village of HECQ and "D" Coy. had particularly bitter fighting.

The three tanks allotted to the Battalion were by this time out of action, but the crew of one tank which had got as far as the T head roads in A.8.b. assisted "C" Coy. considerably by forming a strong point with their Machine Guns.

Ten minutes after ZERO, "A" and "B" Coys. advanced from their forming up positions, and passing through "D" Coy., caught up with the barrage and attacked the WESTERN edge of the FOREST de MORMAL, pushing through to their final objective which they reached to time. A considerable number of the enemy were killed and many prisoners taken.

By 0945 hours HECQ was clear of the enemy and patrols were sent through the Forest to get in touch with "A" and "B" Coys.

At 0915 hours a portion of the 8th. Battalion Royal Berks Regiment continued the attack. By this time the two front Coys. had linked up with the 6th. Battn. Northamptonshire Regiment on the right and the 2nd. Battn. Royal Welsh Fusiliers on the left.

During the morning a party of the enemy about 30 strong and led by two Officers attacked "A" Coy. from the rear. By a cleverly executed flank movement, O.C., "A" Coy. completely rounded up this party, who, when their two Officers had become casualties, surrendered. They were found to be equipped with Machine GUNS and Trench Mortars.

As the attack on the right had been held up, O.C., "A" Coy. swung his left flank on to A.10.c.4.9. with his right resting at A.15.b.1.7. O.C., "B" Coy. conformed to this movement by pushing forward his line, but still keeping in touch with the 2nd. Battn. Royal Welsh Fusiliers on the left.

The Coys. remained in these positions until the following day when the Battalion was concentrated in HECQ.

Contd.

- 2 -

The casualties sustained were :-
2/Lieut. H.S.PEDLAR.   Killed.
2/Lieut. E.FULLER.   Killed.
2/Lieut. P.J.BOLTON.   Wounded, (since died of Wds.)
2/Lieut. E.A.R.HEWITT.   Wounded.
and 46 other ranks.

About 200 prisoners were captured in this operation.

(Signed:-) G.C.TENNSON, Lieut,
Assistant Adjutant,
7th. Battalion Royal West Kent Regiment.

Army Form C. 2118.

WAR DIARY
or
INTELLIGENCE SUMMARY.
(Erase heading not required.)

7 R.W. Kent Nov 1918 Vol 39

Instructions regarding War Diaries and Intelligence Summaries are contained in F. S. Regs., Part II. and the Staff Manual respectively. Title pages will be prepared in manuscript.

Place	Date	Hour	Summary of Events and Information	Remarks and references to Appendices
LINE.	1/3-11-18.		Battalion holding left sector of 53rd. Infantry Brigade front.	
	4-11-18.		Battalion attacked at 0615 hours in conjunction with 54th. Infantry Brigade on right and 2nd. Battalion Welsh Fusiliers on left. All objectives gained. 155- Prisoners taken (including 5- Officers). Casualties:- 4- Officers, 45- O.Rs.	App.158.
	5-11-18.		Battalion withdrawn to Billets in HECQ.	
	6-11-18.		Battalion moved by march route to LE CATEAU, departing 0900 hours, arriving 1600 hours.	App.159.
LE CATEAU.	7/12-11-18.		Battalion in Billets. Training.	
	13-11-18.		Battalion moved by march route to PREMONT, departing 0915 hours, arriving 1600 hours.	App.160.
PREMONT.	14/30-11-18.		Battalion in Billets. Training and Salvage Operations. Educational Training.	

OFFICERS JOINED DURING THE MONTH.

2/Lieut. G.HUMPAGE.   Rejoined 12-11-18.
2/Lieut. C.M.HOLMES.   Joined 18-11-18.
Lieut. F.C.NEEDHAM.   Joined 22-11-18.
Lieut. G.G.F.RICHMOND.   Joined 22-11-18.
2/Lieut. F.J.MORRIS.   Joined 22-11-18.
Lieut. O.J.LONGSTAFF.   Joined 23-11-18.
2/Lieut. T.P.JONES.   Rejoined 23-11-18.
2/Lieut. E.G.HICKS.   Joined 23-11-18.
2/Lieut. J.KINDER.   Joined 23-11-18.

Army Form C. 2118.

WAR DIARY
or
INTELLIGENCE SUMMARY.
(Erase heading not required.)

Instructions regarding War Diaries and Intelligence Summaries are contained in F. S. Regs., Part II. and the Staff Manual respectively. Title pages will be prepared in manuscript.

Place	Date	Hour	Summary of Events and Information	Remarks and references to Appendices
	NOVEMBER. 1918.			

OFFICERS CASUALTIES DURING THE MONTH.

2/Lieut. H.A.DEBENHAM.	Wounded and Missing 1-11-18.	
2/Lieut. H.S.PEGLAR.	Killed in Action 4-11-18.	
2/Lieut. B.FULLER.	Killed in Action 4-11-18.	
2/Lieut. P.J.BOLTON.	Wounded 4-11-18.	
2/Lieut. E.A.R.HEWETT.	Wounded 4-11-18.	
2/Lieut. B.HOWLETT.	Sick to England 23-11-18.	
2/Lieut. A.F.NEILL.	Sick to England 23-11-18.	

HONOURS AND REWARDS.

BAR TO THE MILITARY MEDAL.

21522. L/C. A.E.PHILLIPS, M.M.   Missing 28-10-18.

THE MILITARY MEDAL.

1989. CPL. WAGHORN. C.L.		19026. L/C. WATERHOUSE.E.M.	Wounded 4-11-18.
21362. Cpl. SKELTON. T.A.		21511. Pte. GOLDBERG. S.	Wounded 26-10-18.
38659. Pte. WARREN. F.G.		10515. Pte. LEIGH. F.	Wounded 23-10-18.
18790. Pte. COLBRAN. G.T.		21127. Pte. TAGGART. T.	Evac. 12-11-18.
38705. Pte. COLE. J.	Wounded 24-9-18.	24327. Pte. FIELD. A.	
21513. L/C. ALDRED. A.		10362. L/C. HOOD. E.	

[signature] Lieut. Col.
4th. November, 1918.   Commanding 7th. Battalion Royal West Kent Regiment.

WAR DIARY
or
INTELLIGENCE SUMMARY.

(Erase heading not required.)

Army Form C. 2118.

Place	Date	Hour	Summary of Events and Information	Remarks and references to Appendices
			2nd BAR TO THE MILITARY CROSS.	
			Capt. A.V. McDONALD, M.C.	
			Capt. H.J.M. HARRIS, M.C.	
			BAR TO THE MILITARY CROSS.	
			Lieut. G.G. THOMSON, M.C.	
			Capt. R. MALTBY, M.C.	
			Lieut. H.E. FOSTER, M.C. U.S., M.O.R.C. Attached 7th. Bn. R.W. Kent Regiment.	
			THE MILITARY CROSS.	
			2/Lieut. R.B.L. HILL. Wdd. 24-10-18.	
			2/Lieut. A.B. CULLERNE. Killed 23-10-18.	
			BAR TO THE MILITARY MEDAL.	
			21501. L/Sgt. Sterry. M.J. M.M. D.O. Wds. 27-10-18.	
			202235. Pte. Pigott. F.E. M.M. Killed 19-9-18.	
			THE MILITARY MEDAL.	
			242103. Pte. Wareham. A.W.	
			24849. Pte. Woodcock. W.J.	
			205342. Sgt. Goff. Since to England for Commission.	
			21426. Pte. Cropper. R.	
			201622. Pte. King. A.	
			5938. Pte. Sears. J. Wdd. 24-8-18.	
			202711. Pte. Lock. F.	
			202235. Pte. Pigott. F.E. Killed 19-9-18.	
			204659. Pte. Breeds. H. Evac., Sick 27-8-18.	
			10184. L/C. McCormick. D.	
			206409. Sgt. Kemp. C.	
			21445. A/Sgt. Smith. C.S.	
			242131. Pte. Chillery. J.	
			21531. Cpl. Hoddinott. A.V. Wdd. 22-9-18.	
			THE MILITARY MEDAL. (Continued).	
			266799. Pte. Brooker. M.R. Wdd. 18-9-18.	
			242046. Pte. Moodnick. B.	
			1989. Cpl. Waghorn. C.L.	
			21362. Cpl. Skelton. T.A.	
			38659. Pte. Warren. F.G.	
			18790. Pte. Colbran. G.T. Wdd. 24-9-18.	
			38705. Pte. Cole. J.	
			THE CROIX DE GUERRE and DIPLOMA for GALLANTRY.	
			30944. Cpl. Mellors. P.W.	
7th. November, 1918.				

Major,
Commanding 7th. Battalion Royal West Kent Regiment.

Army Form C. 2118.

WAR DIARY
or
INTELLIGENCE SUMMARY.

(Erase heading not required.)

7 R W Kent
Decr 1918
Vol 40

Instructions regarding War Diaries and Intelligence Summaries are contained in F. S. Regs., Part II. and the Staff Manual respectively. Title pages will be prepared in manuscript.

Place	Date	Hour	Summary of Events and Information	Remarks and references to Appendices
PREMONT.	1-12-18.		Church Services.	
	2-12-18.		Divisional Review by Major-General R.P.LEE, C.B., Commanding 18th. Division.	
	3/7-12-18.		Salvage operations and Educational Training.	
	8-12-18.		- Ditto - Demobilization of Coal Miners commenced.	
	9-12-18.		Salvage operations and Educational Training.	
	10-12-18.		- Ditto - "C" Coy. moved to billets at BEAUREVOIR for salvage work in that area.	
	11/12-12-18.		Salvage operations and Educational Training.	
	13-12-18.		- Ditto - "D" Coy. moved to "SWISS COTTAGE" FARM, H.10.b.3.7. (Ref. Map. 62.B. 1/40,000), near VIANCOURT for salvage work in that area.	
	14/17-12-18.		Salvage operations and Educational Training.	
	18-12-18.		- Ditto - Court of Inquiry held regarding allegations of German Government as to the disposal of Prisoners of War at the SAILLY-SAILLISEL operation on 1-9-18.	APP. 161.
	19/22-12-18.		Salvage operations and Educational Training.	
	23/27-12-18.		Christmas Holidays.	
	28/31-12-18.		Salvage operations and Educational Training.	
			------o0o------	

DECEMBER, 1918. OFFICERS WHO HAVE JOINED DURING THE MONTH.

LIEUT. C.A.W. DUFFIELD, M.C. Re-Joined 2-12-18.

OFFICERS CASUALTIES DURING THE MONTH.

CAPTAIN. A.V. McDONALD, M.C. Taken on Establishment of Fourth Army School from 15-12-18.

2/LIEUT. E.G. HICKS. To ENGLAND to be DEMOBILIZED 18-12-18.

Army Form C. 2118.

WAR DIARY
or
INTELLIGENCE SUMMARY.
(Erase heading not required.)

Instructions regarding War Diaries and Intelligence Summaries are contained in F. S. Regs., Part II. and the Staff Manual respectively. Title pages will be prepared in manuscript.

Place	Date	Hour	Summary of Events and Information	Remarks and references to Appendices
	DECEMBER, 1918.		HONOURS AND REWARDS DURING THE MONTH.	

THE MILITARY CROSS.
T/Capt. (A/Major) F.T. KIRK.
2/Lieut. A.H. OAKLEY.
LIEUT. B.M. OLIVER.
2/LIEUT. G.A. ATTEY.

THE DISTINGUISHED CONDUCT MEDAL.
No.976. Sgt. A. GREGORY.
No.205338. Cpl. J.D. AITCHISON. Wounded 23-10-18.
No.21501. Sgt. L.J. STERRY, M.M. (Died of Wounds 27-10-18.)

BAR TO THE MILITARY MEDAL.
No.18181. Cpl. E. WORSLEY, M.M. (Attached/T.M. Battery.)
53rd.

THE MILITARY MEDAL.
No.18681. L/C. J. ORBELL.
No.21380. Sgt. J. DOWNS.
No.29951. Cpl. W.H.R. DIBBS.
No.265074. Sgt. F.L. DANN.
No.30032. A/Sgt. F.K. ATTENBOROUGH.
No.28718. Pte. J. BROWN.(Attached 53rd. T.M. Battery.)
No.29387. Pte. H. STOCKLEY.
No.18470. L/C. R.L. MARTIN.
No.21521. L/C. J. ERSKINE.
No.28700. Pte. E.F. BARTRICK.
No.10199. L/C. G. PASSEY. Wounded 23-10-18.

-----o0o-----

[signature]
Lieut. Col.
Commanding 7th. Battalion Royal West Kent Regiment.

WAR DIARY
or
INTELLIGENCE SUMMARY.

(Erase heading not required.)

Army Form C. 2118.

F & F.

Place	Date	Hour	Summary of Events and Information	Remarks and references to Appendices
PREMONT.	1-1-19. 2/19-1-19. 20-1-19.		General Holiday. Salvage Operations, Lewis Gun Training and Educational Training. Battalion moved by march route to billets in BERTRY (P.8.d. - Sheet 57.B.). "C" and "D" Coys. rejoined Battalion from BEAUREVOIR and WIANCOURT respectively at CROSS-ROADS - U.21.d.7.9. - Sheet 57.B. Left 1200 hours; arrived 1430 hours.	APP.162.
BERTRY.	21-1-19. 22/30-1-19. 31-1-19.		Battalion Cleaning up and settling into billets. Salvage Operations, Training and Educational Training. Rehearsal for Presentation of Colours.	
			---------o0o---------	

JANUARY, 1919.			OFFICERS JOINED DURING THE MONTH.
			
			    NIL.
			
			OFFICERS CASUALTIES DURING THE MONTH.
			
			    CAPTAIN. R.D.MILLIGAN. Proceeded for Demobilization 21-1-19.
			    LIEUT. B.M.OLIVER, M.C. " " 28-1-19.
			    CAPTAIN. R.MALTBY, M.C. " " 28-1-19.
			    LIEUT. R.F.KNIGHT. " " 25-1-19.
			    2/LIEUT. G.A.OWEN. To ENGLAND, Sick 7-1-19.
			    2/LIEUT. J.KINDER. " " 7-1-19.
			
			HONOURS & REWARDS DURING THE MONTH.
			DISTINGUISHED SERVICE ORDER.
			
			    LIEUT. COLONEL. L.H. HICKSON. } NEW YEARS' HONOURS
			    MAJOR. A.E.PHILLIPS. } GAZETTE.	

Lieut. Col.
Commanding 7th. Battalion Royal West Kent Regiment.

Copy No........

7th. Battalion Royal West Kent Regiment.

OPERATION ORDER NO.90.

Ref. Map.
FRANCE, 57.B.
1/40,000.

19th. January, 1919.

1. The 7th. Battalion Royal West Kent Regiment will move to BERTRY, P.8.d., on MONDAY, 20th. January, 1919.

2. STARTING POINT. The Starting Point will be the Cross-Roads at U.21.d.7.9., which will be passed at 1215 hours.

3. Hd. Qrs., "A" and "B" Coys. will parade in the SERAIN ROAD at 1200 hours in fours facing NORTH.
Head of column will be opposite Battn. Hd. Qrs. Mess.
"C" and "D" Coys. will parade in sufficient time to reach Starting Point at 1215 hours where they will join the Battalion.
Bn.H.Qrs.

4. ORDER OF MARCH. BAND,/"A" and "B", "C" and "D" Coys., Transport.

5. DRESS. Marching Order. Steel Helmets to be attached to Pack by Cross-straps.

6. COOKING ARRANGEMENTS. Hd.Qrs., "A" and"B" Coys. will have dinners at 1115 hours. "C" and "D" Coys. will have dinners en route.

7. Officers' Kits, Blankets, Greatcoats, and Packs & Rifles of BAND will be dumped at Q.M. Stores at 1000 hours.

8. The Mess Cart will collect the Mess Boxes from the Messes at 1130 hrs.

9. TRANSPORT.
2- G.S. Wagons and 2- Limbers will report to "C" Coy.Hd.Qrs. at 0900 hours.
2- G.S. Wagons and 1- Limber will report to "D" Coy.Hd.Qrs. at 0900 hours.
7- G.S. Wagons will be available for carrying Tables, Forms, Beds, Stoves etc., and will be loaded up during the morning.
1- G.S. Wagon is detailed for Orderly Room and Demobilization Office.

10. Officers' Chargers will report to Hd.Qrs. concerned at 1155 hours.

11. O.C. "A" Coy. will detail 1- N.C.O. and 6- men to remain behind at Quartermaster Stores as Guard and Loading Party of any Stores left behind.

12. ACKNOWLEDGE.

(Signed:-) G.G.THOMSON, Capt.,
A/Adjutant,
7th. Battalion Royal West Kent Regiment.

Army Form C. 2118.

WAR DIARY
or
INTELLIGENCE SUMMARY.
(Erase heading not required.)

Instructions regarding War Diaries and Intelligence Summaries are contained in F.S. Regs., Part II. and the Staff Manual respectively. Title pages will be prepared in manuscript.

Place	Date	Hour	Summary of Events and Information	Remarks and references to Appendices
BERTRY.	1/11-2-19. 7-2-19. 8/11-2-19. 12-2-19.		Parades under Company arrangements. Educational & Recreational Training. Presentation of Colours by Corps Commander. Lewis Gun, Educational and Recreational Training. Battalion re-organised into two Companies, "Y" Coy for Army of Occupation, "Z" Coy for Demobilisation.	
	13/25-2-19.		Demobilisation still proceeding. Parades under Coy arrangements for Lewis Gun, Educational and Recreational Training.	
	26-2-19.		Two Officers and 205- O.R. proceeded to join 17th Bn. Royal Sussex Regiment (Army of Occupation.)	
	27/28-2-19.		Personnel for Cadre detailed, Mobilisation stores conveyed to CAUDRY.	

------000------

OFFICERS JOINED DURING THE MONTH.

Lieut. P.D.BERTRAM............ Rejoined from 53rd. T.M.B., 9-2-19.

OFFICERS CASUALTIES DURING THE MONTH.

```
Captain. T.H.SOLOMON............ To U.K., Sick, 30-1-19.
Lieut. C.A.W.DUFFIELD. MC....     -do-         7-2-19.
Captain I.F.S.SPALDING.........  Demobilised, 1-2-19.
2/Lieut. F.AXTELL. MM...........  Retained for Demobilisation whilst on leave in U.K.,
                                  and struck off strength from 23-2-19.
2/Lieut. F.J.MORRIS.............  To U.K., for Demobilisation, 2-2-19.
2/Lieut. E.V.TOZER..............     -do-         13-2-19.
Lieut. A.W.C.WINGFIELD..........     -do-         13-2-19.
Lieut. F.C.NEEDHAM..............     -do-         15-2-19.
Captain. D. G. PHIPPS...........     -do-         16-2-19.
Lieut. O. J. LONGSTAFF..........     -do-         18-2-19.
2/Lieut. G. HUMPAGE.............     -do-         18-2-19.
```

Army Form C. 2118.

WAR DIARY
or
INTELLIGENCE SUMMARY.
(Erase heading not required.)

Instructions regarding War Diaries and Intelligence Summaries are contained in F. S. Regs., Part II. and the Staff Manual respectively. Title pages will be prepared in manuscript.

Place	Date	Hour	Summary of Events and Information	Remarks and references to Appendices
BERTRY.	FEBRUARY. 1919.		OFFICERS CASUALTIES DURING THE MONTH (Contd.)	
			Captain A.V.D.MORLEY, MC..... Proceeded to join 17th Bn. ROYAL SUSSEX REGT., (Army of Occupation), 26-2-19.	
			Lieut. G.G.F.RICHMOND........ -do-	
			HONOURS & REWARDS ANNOUNCED DURING MONTH.	
			Mentioned in Despatches...... Lieut. Col. L.H.HICKSON, D.S.O.	
			Major A.E.PHILLIPS, D.S.O.	
			Military Medal............... No. 21481. Pte. Lucas. F.J.	

                                                       Commanding 7th Battalion Royal West Kent Regiment.

Army Form C. 2118.

7 R W Kent

WAR DIARY
or
INTELLIGENCE SUMMARY.
(Erase heading not required.)

Instructions regarding War Diaries and Intelligence Summaries are contained in F. S. Regs., Part II. and the Staff Manual respectively. Title pages will be prepared in manuscript.

Place	Date	Hour	Summary of Events and Information	Remarks and references to Appendices
BERTRY.	1-3-19.		Battalion moved by March Route to CLARY. Start, 14.00 hrs; arrived 14.45 hrs.	App. 163
CLARY.	2/30-3-19.		Battalion in Billets at CLARY. Demobilisation proceeding; available personnel being despatched to 17th ROYAL SUSSEX REGT., (Army of Occupation).	
	31-3-19.		Battalion now reduced to Cadre "A" strength.	
			OFFICERS JOINED DURING THE MONTH.	
			Major W.R.STEWART (E.Surrey Regt)., joined to assume Command of Cadre, 28-3-19.	
			OFFICERS CASUALTIES DURING THE MONTH.	
			Major A.F.NORTHCOTE. To U.K. for service with Regt. abroad, 5-3-19.	
			2/Lieut. R.H.PIGOU. -do- -do- 6-3-19.	
			2/Lieut. F.G.NORRIS. -do- -do- 28-3-19.	
			2/Lieut. C.S.TURNER. To join 6th Bn. R.W.Kent Regt. 20-3-19.	
			2/Lieut. G.A.ATTEY. M.C. -do- -do- 20-3-19.	
			2/Lieut. T.S.LEEMING. -do- -do- 20-3-19.	
			Capt. H.J.M.HARRIS. M.C. To U.K. for Demobilisation. 27-2-19.	
			Major F.T.KIRK. M.C. -do- -do- 7-3-19.	
			2/Lieut. A.W.JONES. -do- -do- 10-3-19.	
			------------o0o------------	
			W R Stewart. Major.	
			Commanding 7th Bn. Royal West Kent Regiment.	

APP 163

Copy No.........

7th. Battalion Royal West Kent Regiment.

OPERATION ORDERS No. 91.

Ref. Map.
FRANCE. 57.B.
1/40,00

28th. February. 1919

1. The 7th Battalion Royal West Kent Regiment will move to CLARY O.17.d on SATURDAY, 1st March, 1919.

2. The Battalion will parade at 1400 hours in Main Road in fours facing South. Head of Column to be opposite Bn. Orderly Room.
COLOURS. Colours will be carried cased by 2/Lieut. W.A.SHEARING with an escort of 1 Sergt. and 2 Other Ranks.

3. DRESS. Marching Order.

4. Officers Kits, Orderly Room and Demobilization Boxes will be collected at 1100 hours.
Blankets will be rolled and dumped at Q.M.Stores at 0900 hours,.

5. Mess Cart will collect Mess Boxes from Officers Messes at 1400 hours and will follow the Battalion to CLARY.

6. COOKING ARRANGEMENTS. Dinners will be served at 1200 hours.

7. TRANSPORT. 4 Lorries will report at Q.M.Stores at 0900 hours for carrying Blankets, Tables, Forms, Beds, etc.

8. Billets will be left in a clean state and will be inspected by an Officer of Z Coy. at 1345 hours, who will report afterwards to the Adjutant.

9. ACKNOWLEDGE.

(Signed:) G.G.THOMSON, Capt.,
A/Adjutant.
7th. Battalion Royal West Kent Regiment.

Copies to:-
1. C.O.
2. Adjutant.
3. O.C. Z.Coy.
4. Q.M. & T.O.
5. R.S.M.

WAR DIARY or INTELLIGENCE SUMMARY.

Army Form C. 2118.

7 R W Kents

Place	Date	Hour	Summary of Events and Information	Remarks and references to Appendices
CLARY.	1/30-4-19.		Battalion Cadre in Billets.	
			OFFICERS JOINED DURING MONTH.	
			NIL.	
			OFFICERS CASUALTIES DURING MONTH.	
			Lieut. G.C.S.BASKETT. Demobilised whilst on Leave in U.K., 10-3-19.	
			Lieut. C.M.HOLMES. To 6th Bn.R.W.Kent Regt. 2-4-19.	
			2/Lieut. W.G.BARRETT. -do- 2-4-19.	
			2/Lieut. A.H.OAKLEY. M.C. -do- 2-4-19.	
			2/Lieut. G.A.STAPLEY. M.M. -do- 2-4-19.	
			Lieut. T.P.JONES. -do- 4-4-19.	
			Lieut. W.A.SHEARING. -do- 11-4-19.	
			2/Lieut. H.J.TURNER. -do- 19-4-19.	

A.H. Boper Rey
Captain.
Commanding 7th Battalion Royal West Kent Regiment Cadre.

www.ingramcontent.com/pod-product-compliance
Lightning Source LLC
Chambersburg PA
CBHW081428160426
43193CB00013B/2218